X Child Stars

X Child Stars

Where Are They Now?

KATHY GARVER
AND
FRED ASCHER

TAYLOR TRADE PUBLISHING
Lanham • Boulder • New York • London

TAYLOR TRADE PUBLISHING
An imprint of Rowman & Littlefield

Distributed by NATIONAL BOOK NETWORK

British Library Cataloguing in Publication Information Available

Library of Congress Cataloging-in-Publication Data Available

ISBN 978-1-63076-113-4 (hardback)
ISBN 978-1-63076-114-1 (e-book)

∞™ The paper used in this publication meets the minimum requirements of American National Standard for Information Sciences—Permanence of Paper for Printed Library Materials, ANSI/NISO Z39.48-1992.

Printed in the United States of America

This book is lovingly dedicated to one of the most famous child stars of all time, the tiny but largely talented Shirley Temple.

Contents

CONTENTS

CONTENTS

CONTENTS

CONTENTS

CONTENTS

CONTENTS

CONTENTS

CONTENTS

CONTENTS

CONTENTS

Foreword

I have been tracking the "child star syndrome" for almost forty years, and my main takeaway is that it is not "we" who change so much as it is the "audience" that watched us grow up.

It's fair to say that no one has more "former child star" friends than I, nor has anyone followed them more closely over the decades. For example, Tony Dow (*Leave It to Beaver*) and I have been friends for more than fifty years. Jay North (he played Dennis in *Dennis the Menace*) and I have been pals for nearly fifty-five years. The foundation my wife and I started back in 1990, A Minor Consideration, has more than eight hundred members, and Kathy Garver is a charter member.

Nearly all of us are like the proverbial "bug trapped in amber" made famous by *Jurassic Park*. Our lives have proceeded apace, but those who watched us as children on television or in movies cling to old images of us while they, understandably, have gone on with their lives. They've changed, but their apprehension of us . . . as people . . . has not. And therein lies the trouble.

I understand fads. I was one. In my own life I have a certain fondness for hula hoops, roller skates, and ancient infatuations with girls I loved and lost . . . but I respect those memories. The images we as a group created, however, fall into a different category because all too often we fall victim to your "I grew past those old 'infatuations'" syndrome, as if the erstwhile fondness is no longer relevant, and thus becomes something to dismiss . . . with prejudice.

If you have a younger brother or sister, you know how easily they avoid caring about what their older sibling finds fascinating. That's the way of the world.

It's one thing to have a complete stranger walk up to you and say, "Hey, didn't you used to be somebody?" and quite another to have someone say, "Gee, I used to love you."

It's okay to continue to have affection and respect for the idols of your childhood. Growing up doesn't have to mean that you turn your back on the kids you found appealing. We are all connected to our childhood years. For better or worse, we are tied to each other.

Kid stars will always be a part of the entertainment industry. How they turn out depends on many factors, with good fortune being the larger part of adult success. You will read how some of these lives have turned out, and I hope you absorb these tales with a degree of loyalty and respect.

A Minor Consideration has become the home for many of these former kid stars who span the entire history of show business. Kathy worked hard on this compendium, and I hope you enjoy the read.

Paul Petersen

Founder, A Minor Consideration

Introduction

When my friend Kathy Garver and I first discussed my involvement in writing a book about ex–child stars, what piqued her interest in me and what stood out from other pitches she had heard over the years was why I thought a book like this was needed. I don't see these former actors as washed-out has-beens who provide fodder for throwaway gossip magazines. And I don't look at the child stars listed in this book as curiosities from previous eras. On the contrary, to me they comprise one of our most precious national treasures.

Nearly everyone reading this page grew up in post–World War II America, and at least one-third of us were latchkey kids who returned from school to empty houses because both our parents worked outside the home. When we came home from school, we weren't really alone. We would flip on the TV and spend the afternoon with our most loyal friends: the child stars.

This book only scratches the surface of all the biographies we wanted to include. We believe you'll love this edition so much you'll want a sequel, and I know Kathy would be delighted to oblige! In this book you'll discover the fates of many of your favorite childhood stars, from the truly tragic to the super successful and everything in between. Some of the ex–child stars aren't ex-stars at all—think of Ron Howard, Leonardo DiCaprio, and Christina Applegate, who all began as child stars on television.

Some of the ex–child stars may no longer be stars as defined by Ron or Leo, but they have been quite successful in adulthood. My coauthor, Kathy Garver, along with Alison Arngrim, Melissa Gilbert, Joey Lawrence, and many others, figure in this group.

What saddens me—and what inspired me to create this book with Kathy—is the overblown interest the press and its audience take in reading about troubled ex–child stars. I think that this pleasure may come from a place of envy—seeing someone fall from grace whose fame we once coveted. Or maybe it is morbid curiosity. In any case, we have included the tragic stories, too, but we hope that we have respectfully told the stories of those who have had hardships. Kathy has proudly written about many ex–child stars who seemed to be in a helpless downward spiral of drugs and abuse but were able to turn their lives around, and recover, and thrive.

And the really tragic endings—like the severe drug overdose that took the life of Kathy's *Family Affair* costar Anissa Jones at the age of eighteen—are written as cautionary tales with respect to those we've lost without passing judgment on the choices that often lead to an early grave.

The day I first met Kathy was at a celebrity signing event near LAX. I remember entering a room filled with many famous stars of yesteryear, including June Lockhart, Barbara Eden, and Pat Boone, among others. Sitting in the corner by the front door at a small wooden table were Brian Forster and Suzanne Crough from *The Partridge Family*. I was struck by how small their table was; it seemed almost disrespectful that those two ex–child stars were denied the red carpet treatment they deserved for all those afternoons they were there for us in our otherwise empty house.

It is particularly poignant to me to think of Suzanne Crough's relatively early death in 2015. She was one of the people who inspired me to write this book and begin a movement to hold our ex–child stars up to a new light. I only wish she had lived to see the fruits of her inspiration.

Fred Ascher

July 1, 2015

THE 1950s

I Love Lucy /
The Lucy-Desi Comedy Hour

9 Seasons: 180 half-hour *I Love Lucy* episodes (1951–57), 13 one-hour *The Lucy-Desi Comedy Hour* episodes (1957–60), and one unaired 30-minute pilot (1951)

Network: CBS; All episodes black and white

Debut: October 15, 1951 / Finale: April 30, 1960

It is appropriate that the first major child star rose to fame on the show that built the mold for all the sitcoms to follow: *I Love Lucy*. When it premiered in October 1951, television was in its infancy. Indeed, many cities were still waiting for broadcast television to arrive; some areas had to wait well into the decade. This fact makes the size of the audience on the night Lucy gave birth to Little Ricky, January 19, 1953, all the more amazing. It was the night before President Dwight D. Eisenhower would be sworn in (and truly usher in "the '50s"). By coincidence, Lucille Ball gave birth in real life to Desi Arnaz Jr. as Lucy Ricardo brought Little Ricky into the world. More than 71 percent of America's television sets—a higher percentage than those who watched President Eisenhower take the oath of office—were tuned in to learn the gender of the Ricardo baby. The simple premise of a popular bandleader fending off his clever, redheaded spouse's efforts to "be in the show," with the aid of best friends and neighbors Fred and Ethel, continues to stir America's imagination to this day. Little Keith Thibodeaux, America's first television child star, will forever be remembered as the iconic Little Ricky.

Keith Thibodeaux and Lucille Ball on the set of *I Love Lucy*.
CBS/Photofest

KEITH THIBODEAUX

(Born December 1, 1950)

Character: Little Ricky Ricardo

A drumming prodigy, billed on *I Love Lucy* as Richard Keith, was "Little Ricky," pint-sized sidekick to dad Ricky Ricardo (Desi Arnaz). Keith was discovered by Lucille and Desi as the boy was touring with the Horace Heidt Orchestra, which he had been doing since the age of two. Keith segued to *The Lucy-Desi Comedy Hour* in 1957. He appeared in other TV shows, most notably *The Andy Griffith Show,* where he played Opie's pal until he quit acting in 1966. Keith continued to play drums, but he succumbed to drugs when he was playing with the rock group David and the Giants. The band broke up, but Keith, as he noted in his book, *Life after Lucy,* found Christ and gave up drugs. The band eventually reconvened and released almost ten albums in the 1980s and 1990s. In 2014 they recorded a live CD entitled *Still Rockin'.* Keith now runs Ballet Magnificat!, his wife Kathy's Christian ballet company, and they have one daughter, Tara, a talented dancer and choreographer.

The Adventures of Ozzie and Harriet

14 Seasons: 425 half-hour episodes—the most episodes of a live-action sitcom in television history

Network: ABC; Seasons 1–13, black and white; Season 14, color

Debut: October 3, 1952 / Finale: March 26, 1966

The longest-running sitcom in television history so far actually began on the radio in 1944 with the sons of stars Ozzie and Harriet Nelson joining the radio cast before the end of that decade. The Nelsons' "adventures" were usually mundane by today's standards. But it was postwar America, and viewers, having survived the Great Depression and saved democracy in World War II, were interested in building families, neighborhoods in the suburbs, and a semblance of normalcy. Ozzie and Harriet were the perfect role models for peacetime America, and their boys reflected the values that all parents wished for their children. Simplistic? Absolutely. As the boys grew and married on the show, the world of the Nelsons remained insulated from presidential assignations, civil rights marches, and cultural upheaval. A revival attempt in the mid-1970s was short-lived, proving the Nelsons, a cornerstone of American entertainment for nearly a quarter of a century, had become a treasured relic of the past.

RICKY NELSON

(May 8, 1940–December 31, 1985)
Character: Ricky Nelson

Eric Nelson, known to the world as "Ricky," started in the show business world on his parents' radio show, *The Adventures of Ozzie and Harriet*, when he was eight years old. After two years, he moved into the television version of the series, which ran for twelve years and on which he became a teen idol. When the TV series ended, Ricky became "Rick," and he continued his musical endeavors with the Stone Canyon Band. In 1963 he married Kristin Harmon and they had four children: Tracy, Matthew, and the twins Gunnar and Sam. His use of drugs has been well documented. He began with marijuana and went on to cocaine and quaaludes. Rick's habitual drug abuse was one of the reasons the couple was divorced in 1982. The talented ex–child star, teen idol, and successful singer-songwriter was unfortunately killed in a plane crash in 1985 on his way to perform in Texas.

DAVID NELSON

(October 24, 1936–January 11, 2011)
Character: David Nelson

David, the older son of Ozzie and Harriet, also began on the radio version of *The Adventures of Ozzie and Harriet*. When the television show ended, David produced *Ozzie's Girls* in 1973, which lasted one year in syndication. David continued to produce and then direct, creating commercials, TV shows, and films. In 1961 he married ex–*Playboy*-playmate-of-the-month June Blair. The couple had two children, Daniel and James, before they were divorced in 1975. David married Yvonne Huston in 1975 and adopted her three children. Recalling his experiences on the show, David once said, "It's an awful big load to carry, to be everyone's fantasy family." He died at age seventy-five of colon cancer while living in Century City, Los Angeles.

Our Miss Brooks

4 Seasons: 130 half-hour episodes
Network: CBS; All episodes black and white
Debut: October 3, 1952 / Finale: May 11, 1956

Our Miss Brooks was, like *The Adventures of Ozzie and Harriet*, a radio hit that transitioned to television. Unlike the Nelsons' program, however, the high school hijinks of Miss Brooks and her zany cast of teenagers and faculty seemed to work better in the theatre of the mind than through the magic of the new visual medium. The series was a big hit on the radio beginning in the late 1940s, and it continued to broadcast new episodes on the radio throughout its television run. In fact, *Our Miss Brooks* remained on the radio for one additional season, 1956–1957, after the television show had folded after four seasons.

GLORIA McMILLAN

(Born March 13, 1936)

Character: Harriet Conklin

Gloria's mother, Hazel McMillan, was the first female theatrical agent and this author's representative for over twelve years. Through Hazel, Gloria started her career in radio when she was a four-year-old; that experience helped land her the part of Harriet Conklin on the radio show, *Our Miss Brooks*. Gloria continued her role as Harriet when Eve Arden's sardonic sitcom took to the small screen. After a few more roles in television, Gloria resumed playing the radio circuit and appeared in some later TV shows such as *Dr. Kildare*. But she primarily put her theatrical expertise to good use by opening a performing arts studio in San Bernardino, which she and her husband run.

The Life of Riley

6 Seasons: 217 half-hour episodes

Network: NBC; All episodes black and white

Debut: January 2, 1953 / Finale: May 23, 1958

The Life of Riley was a popular radio program in the 1940s, and there was even one season of the sitcom as a TV program starring Jackie Gleason in 1949. But the version most fondly remembered stars William Bendix as the title character. The show was a staple in syndication throughout the 1950s and 1960s, and while it has since fallen into obscurity, it is still common to hear the expression that someone is living "the life of Riley," the expression on which the show's title was based. "Life of Riley" refers to someone who has an easygoing life, which Bendix's character did have, but not for the reasons one would assume. Week after week, Riley would weave from one scheme to another with one of his buddies, only to manage to resolve his misadventure before suffering the wrath of his loving but wary wife and family.

LUGENE SANDERS

(Born September 17, 1934)

Character: Barbara "Babs" Riley

Lugene started her career when she moved from her birthplace in Oklahoma City to Los Angeles. She had grabbed the starring role in *Meet Corliss Archer,* a series that lasted only one summer, before she became Babs, the daughter of Chester Riley. She remained with the series for all six seasons but had very few roles afterward. She retired for good in 1960 to raise her two children by Marvin Solomon, whom she married in 1960. They are both now retired and are living in California. Lugene has said that she enjoyed her career as a child star.

WESLEY MORGAN

(Born March 19, 1939)

Character: Junior Riley

Wesley began his acting career with a role in the film *The Miracle of Our Lady of Fatima,* followed by a TV role on *The Schlitz Playhouse*, but he enjoyed fame in his portrayal of Junior on the beloved *The Life of Riley*. He often heard his blustery father exclaim the show's famous and fondly remembered line, "What a revoltin' development this is!" But Junior kept his easy demeanaor. As one of the first child actors turned teenager in a TV sitcom, Wesley helped set the stage for the type of family TV audiences would embrace for years. Wesley earned entry into the Young Hollywood Hall of Fame in 1954. But after his career-defining role, he soon left the show business world. Now he pursues a more private and quiet life—a good development, he says.

Make Room for Daddy / The Danny Thomas Show / Make Room for Granddaddy

12 Seasons (including *Granddaddy* series): 375 total half-hour episodes, with 120 on ABC under the *Make Room for Daddy* title, 231 on CBS as *The Danny Thomas Show*, and 24 more back on ABC as *Make Room for Granddaddy*

Network: ABC 1953–57; CBS 1957–64; ABC 1970–71; All episodes black and white except for the final 24, color episodes of revival series *Make Room for Granddaddy*

Debut (Original): September 29, 1953 / Finale (Original): April 27, 1964

Debut (*Granddaddy*): September 23, 1970 / Finale (*Granddaddy*): March 18, 1971

The story of the series commonly known as *Make Room for Daddy* is the stuff of which television legends are born. It was originally conceived as a series about the impact of the frequent absence of a traveling professional entertainer "daddy" (Danny Thomas as Danny Williams) on his wife and children, who are left to fend for themselves. The series was an early hit on the then–third-wheel network ABC. Jean Hagen played Thomas's annoyed wife, with Sherry Jackson and Rusty Hamer cast as the children. Some say comedy is often funny because it reflects real-life, and this was true of the first years of *Make Room for Daddy*. Hagen and Thomas were often at odds with each other personally, offscreen, and their on-camera chemistry was based on more of a relationship built on conflict than love. When Hagen's contract was up for renewal after Season 3, Thomas declined to renew it, and his character began the fourth year as a widower. By the end of that season, he was engaged to a new love interest played by Marjorie Lord, who would remain his onscreen wife for the remainder of the series's run. But it was almost not to be.

While ratings remained healthy in the fourth season, ABC declined to renew it for a fifth year. CBS eagerly picked up the series, feeling Danny Thomas was the perfect complement to their stable of superstars and TV legends. The name of the show was changed to *The Danny Thomas Show* to distinguish it from the ABC original and establish Lord as a more loving companion to Thomas. While the program kept its new title for the remaining seven years of the original run, the show went to syndication as *Make Room for Daddy*, and that name stuck. When ABC attempted to revive the series, it naturally returned to the program's familiar name and called the revival *Make Room for Granddaddy*.

The appeal of the long-running show is a tribute not only to the very clever and well-casted child stars but also to the program's ability to grow and evolve as it aged and times changed. An interesting sidenote is that the Williams family and the Ricardos of *I Love Lucy* fame guest-starred on each other's programs in the late 1950s, and Lucille Ball made another appearance as the Williams' longtime friend, Lucy Carter (the title character on *Here's Lucy*), on the revival series. Though this last crossover spanned two networks and featured a "different" Lucy character, the reunion was one of the better episodes of that final season.

From left: Sherry Jackson, Danny Thomas, Louise Beavers, Jean Hagen, and Rusty Hamer on the set of *Make Room for Daddy*.

ABC/Photofest

SHERRY JACKSON

(Born February 15, 1942)

Character: Terry Williams

As Danny Thomas and Jean Hagen's daughter, Sherry fulfilled the big sister role to feisty Rusty Hamer with appeal and aplomb. As a small child, she had worked in many TV shows and movies where her talent shone, as in *Trouble Along the Way,* as

John Wayne's daughter, and in *The Miracle of Our Lady of Fatima*. After three years on *The Danny Thomas Show*, she was turning into a voluptuous teen and also getting tired of the series. Her best friend on the show, Jean Hagen, left, but Sherry stayed to finish the last two years of her contract. After the series, she appeared in many TV shows and movies in the '60s and '70s, and cultivated an image as a sexy leading lady. After her love, multimillionaire Fletcher Jones, died in an airplane accident in 1971, Sherry sued for palimony, but she lost. She left show business for good in 1982. The still beautiful Sherry occasionally appears at autograph conventions, but she has put her childhood career, and her sexy struggle to overcome it, to bed.

RUSTY HAMER

(February 15, 1947–January 18, 1990)
Character: Rusty Williams

Hamer began his career at five, and the next year hit TV series gold with *Make Room for Daddy*. Rusty grew up in front of millions as Rusty Williams, the son of the famous Danny Thomas character, exchanging quips and holding his own in the seasoned comedian's presence. As is often the case, it was difficult for Rusty to find other roles after the popular show ended. Although he was cast in occasional TV spots after the show and appeared for the one-season *Make Room for Granddaddy*, it was not enough to sustain a career in the entertainment field. Rusty ran out of money and fled Hollywood. Going home to Louisiana where his mother and brother were living, he worked at odd jobs but became increasingly depressed and in pain from a back ailment. Broke and living in a trailer, he died in 1990 by a self-inflicted gunshot wound. His brother is quoted as saying, "I've heard of a lot of child actors who have become unhappy with their lives after they left the industry." Rusty's death was reportedly the inspiration for the founding of the nonprofit organization A Minor Consideration by Paul Petersen (*The Donna Reed Show*) to help child actors make the adjustment to adulthood from their stardom and celebrity as youngsters.

ANGELA CARTWRIGHT

(Born September 9, 1952)
Character: Linda Williams

Angela was a darling little girl with a happy smile; she was just right to play Danny Thomas's stepdaughter. Before this long-lasting role, she had impressive film credits with Paul Newman (*Somebody Up There Likes Me*) and Sidney Poitier (*Something of Value*). When the series ended, she went on to another classic, the film *The Sound of Music*, where she played the role of Brigitta Von Trapp. Her role in that classic movie made her an icon. Angela then garnered the role of Penny in TV's *Lost in Space*. When that series ended, Angela played occasional roles in episodic TV, but she found her greatest role to be that of raising her family of two children with Steve Gullion, to whom she has been married since 1976. She also discovered an artistic outlet in photography and creating materials and clothing using the imprint of her photographic images. She has coauthored four books and continues to act occasionally and happily make personal appearances.

Annie Oakley

4 Seasons: 81 half-hour episodes

Network: Syndicated; All episodes black and white

Debut: January 1, 1954 / Finale: February 1, 1957

Westerns were really big in the 1950s—huge, in fact. There were only three television networks at the time and a few independent stations sprinkled throughout the country (and no cable or satellite!), but the demand for Westerns was such that there were literally dozens of series on the air. *Annie Oakley* is unique in that genre because the program focused on the adventures of a woman who could outshoot any man and rode a horse named Target. The show is in the public domain now, so several episodes can be found on DVD. The popularity of the show at the time spawned books of "Authorized TV Adventures" and a Dell comic book series.

JIMMY HAWKINS

(Born November 13, 1941)

Character: Tagg Oakley

From the classic *It's a Wonderful Life* in which Jimmy played Tommy, the Bailey's four-year-old son, to the classic *Annie Oakley* in which Jimmy played Tagg, Annie Oakley's brother, this talented child star's career has been filled with quality projects. Jimmy continued to find excellent roles in the sixties such as the regular role of Fennimore Cooper in *Bringing up Buddy*, Johnathan Baylor in *Ichabod and Me,* and Scotty in his film mother's series, *The Donna Reed Show*. His last appearance was in *Kolchak: The Night Stalker,* billed as Jim Hawkins. After his acting career, Jim became a producer and created many TV-movies, including Gary Coleman's *Scout's Honor,* and *Evel Knievel*. Dropping his producer's hat, he donned a hard hat to start the construction and contracting business in which he is still engaged. Not letting a good film lie fallow, he has written five books on *It's a Wonderful Life,* including *It's a Wonderful Life for Kids* and *Favorite Scenes from the Classic Film . . . It's a Wonderful Life*. Not only was this actor able to make a transition and an adjustment to adult life, but he retained fond memories of his child stardom.

Rocky Jones, Space Ranger

2 Seasons: 39 half-hour episodes

Network: Syndicated; All episodes black and white

Debut: February 23, 1954 / Finale: November 16, 1954

Besides Westerns, another popular genre in the 1950s was the "space opera"—science fiction for the young—with larger-than-life heroes and their wide-eyed young sidekicks. Then there were the special effects that seemingly made no attempt to hide the wires or convince viewers that they were seeing a spaceship and not the Christmas ornament that was used as the prop for the show's vehicle. What makes this series stand out is that it was filmed, not aired live or saved on substandard kinescope. Additionally, for their day, the stories were reasonably well written and the special effects were not awful! You can probably find this on DVD and on YouTube if you look for it!

From left: Sally Mansfield, Robert Lyden, and Richard Crane (as Rocky Jones) on the set of *Rocky Jones, Space Ranger*.
Official Films Television/Photofest

ROBERT LYDEN

(May 28, 1942–January 17, 1986)
Character: Bobby

Robert had a short career as a child actor but left a legacy of entertainment. He first appeared in some movies, including *I'll See You in My Dreams* with Doris Day and Danny Thomas, before he starred as Bobby, the space cadet. He acted in more episodics and ended his career in the film *Man of A Thousand Faces,* in which he played Creighton Chaney at thirteen. He married Thelma Sanchez when he was twenty-five, and they had one daughter. When he and Thelma divorced, Bob married an airline hostess. He found work in the real estate mortgage business and was quite successful. Bob died way too young, at age forty-three. Robert never returned to acting as an adult; he had no interest in doing so, as at least one of his best friends could attest.

Lassie

19 Seasons: 571 half-hour episodes

Network: CBS 1954–71; Syndicated 1971–73; Seasons 1–10, black and white; all remaining seasons, color

Debut: September 12, 1954 / **Finale:** March 24, 1973

The story of the heroic collie Lassie spans decades. It appeared weekly on television for nearly twenty years and has been the subject of films, TV specials, and direct-to-DVD productions in the years since the series folded. Lassie helped make collies among the most sought-after dogs in the mid-twentieth century, and the series evolved and changed with the times. Despite its many years on the air, the most popular and frequently repeated seasons are the first ten; Lassie lived with three families over the course of that decade and bonded with the boys in each family. Cloris Leachman took over from Jan Clayton, and then it was the legendary June Lockhart who became the iconic mother to little Timmy Martin. When she saw Lassie barking and running toward her without the company of her son, she knew the dog was definitely "trying to tell me something!" The timeless adventures of Lassie remain relevant to this day.

Lassie the Dog and Tommy Rettig (as Jeff Miller).
CBS/Photofest

TOMMY RETTIG

(December 10, 1941–February 15, 1996)
Character: Jeff Miller

Annie Get your Gun proved to be Tommy's lead-in to the theatrical industry. He was offered more stage roles after his twenty-two-month tour with Mary Martin, but his mother opted for the movie route. That proved to be successful, as he starred in many movies in the '50s including *The 5,000 Fingers of Doctor T*. That appearance got the notice of the producers of *Lassie,* and when the dog himself chose Tommy—Lassie trotted over to him as he stood in the group of the last three hopefuls—his fate was sealed. After the series, Tommy worked in more movies and episodics but strove "just to be a normal kid." His arrests for growing and smoking marijuana didn't help his quest. He graduated from University High, in Los Angeles, in my brother Lance's class, and Lance has said he was a personable fellow. In 1959, Tommy married a girl of fifteen; they had two children and later divorced. Tommy struggled to find work and tried managing a health club. His intelligence shone through when he became intrigued by computers and developed many popular software programs. He died of a heart attack in Marina del Rey, California, at fifty-five. He is quoted as saying, "More than anything, I wanted to be normal. I wanted to have friends, go out on dates—just lead a normal life." But really, what is normal?

JON PROVOST

(Born March 12, 1950)

Character: Timmy Claussen

Jon took over the role of the child on *Lassie* after George Cleveland, another star of the show, died in the middle of the fourth season. Tommy had left, and the producers sought to revamp the concept with a younger version of Tommy. They needed another small boy who also loved dogs to carry on the tradition, and they found him in adorable towheaded Jon. He had already appeared in many popular movies, including *So Big* and *The Country Girl,* with Bing Crosby and Grace Kelly. After the series, at age fourteen, he started appearing in episodics and movies. But then it was time to go college at Sonoma State, and Northern California stole his heart. He decided not to return to Hollywood after he attained a degree in Psychology. He married Sandra Goosens in 1979, and they had two children, Ryan and Katy. They were divorced in 1993. Jon then married Hollywood historian Laurie Jacobson, who wrote his biography, *Timmy's in the Well*. After he retired as a loan broker, Jon began appearing on TV interviews and shows to discuss pop culture, the treatment of children and animals, and what it is like to be an American icon. He is an apt spokesperson for ex–child stars; he's very familiar with their pressures, joys, and "sex, drugs, and rock and roll" environment. Jon made an apt adjustment to adulthood, and his successful career has been confirmed with his star on the Walk of Fame in Hollywood, which he received in 1994.

Father Knows Best

6 Seasons: 203 half-hour episodes

Network: CBS 1954–55; NBC 1955–58; CBS 1958–60; All episodes black and white

Debut: October 3, 1954 / Finale: May 23, 1960

Father Knows Best made a successful transition from radio to television in 1954. The only character to transition from the original cast was father Robert Young, but the rest of the cast immediately endeared itself to America. Many citizens associate the idealism of the 1950s with *Father Knows Best*. An insurance man by day, family man Jim Anderson would arrive home in time to solve the domestic problems of his loving work-at-home wife and their three children. No matter the situation, one knew the episode would end sentimentally while underscoring the fact that father did—as always—know best!

The Anderson Family from *Father Knows Best*. Top row, from left: Elinor Donahue, Robert Young, Jane Wyatt. Bottom row, from left: Lauren Chapin, Billy Gray, 1962.
ABC

LAUREN CHAPIN

(Born May 23, 1945)

Character: Kathy "Kitten" Anderson

Lauren had a couple of TV credits and some show business experience before she was selected from seventy-eight other hopefuls for the series, and she had watched the theatrical antics of her brothers Michael and Billy, who were also child actors. I worked with Billy and Michael on the classic film noir *The Night of the Hunter*, and I saw how talent ran in the family. But after Lauren's series ended, she was ill prepared to carry on with the acting tradition and has said, "I was feeling really self-conscious and getting pimples." Her mother was an alcoholic, and Lauren had little guidance. She dropped out of high school and married at sixteen. Lauren started taking diet pills, and her use soared to sixty pills a day. When she was eligible for her $90,000 in trust-fund money, her mother sued her, and Lauren wound up with only $19,000. Divorced from a second husband by then, she started taking speed, acid, and heroin; she paid for her habit by becoming a woman of the streets. After a term in jail for forgery, followed by rehabilitation, she joined her brother Michael's household and became a born-again Christian. Lauren now leads tours to the Holy Land, manages actors and singers—her daughter Summer is one of her clients—and advises on the dos and don'ts of child acting. In her book, *Father Does Know Best—The Lauren Chapin Story*, she outlines the dangers that can and do befall ex–child actors. Lessons well learned.

BILLY GRAY

(Born January 13, 1938)
Character: James "Bud" Anderson Jr.

Born to an actress, Billy appeared at an early age in movies with his mother, Beatrice Gray. When he was cast in *Father Knows Best*, he already had amassed many excellent credits, including roles in *The Seven Little Foys* and the sci-fi film *The Day the Earth Stood Still.* But Billy was not one for standing still, and he sought additional thrills in motorcycle racing. He had more roles later in his career such as in *Alfred Hitchcock Presents* and *The Greatest Show on Earth*, but he primarily followed his creative bent by inventing useful consumer products such as guitar picks and massagers. As a businessperson he created the successful company BigRock Engineering. He was arrested in 1962 for possession of marijuana, and claims have been made that the adverse notoriety affected his entertainment career and made it difficult to obtain more roles. Billy criticized *Father Knows Best,* the show for which he was best known, and expounded on the fact that the series depicted an unreal situation for a family. He has said, "You know best." He was divorced twice.

The Adventures of Rin Tin Tin

5 Seasons: 166 half-hour episodes

Network: ABC; All episodes black and white

Debut: October 15, 1954 / Finale: May 8, 1959

More popular than *Lassie* in the grand lens of history, brave German shepherd Rin Tin Tin's adventures date back to 1922, during the silent movie serial era. Rin Tin Tin was immensely popular as he helped keep little orphan Rusty alive while being raised by the US Cavalry at the post Fort Apache. The premise was simple: Rin Tin Tin would help the soldiers establish order in the Old West while keeping the whole gaggle of them out of trouble, often just in the nick of time!

The main cast from *Rin Tin Tin*. From left: Lee Aaker, Rin Tin Tin, James Brown, Joe Sawyer, 1956.
Robert R. Blanch

LEE AAKER

(Born September 24, 1943)

Character: Rusty

When he was four years old, Lee was singing and dancing at local clubs at the behest of his mother, who ran a children's theatre academy. It seemed only natural for Lee to take the next step into acting. After being cast in TV episodics, commercials, and even a costarring role with John Wayne in the movie *Hondo,* blond-haired Lee jumped into the action-packed series *Rin Tin Tin,* which had found fame and audience as a radio serial. After five years on the series, he did more episodics and was general assistant to Herbert Leonard (*Route 66*) as a location scout. He was married for two years to Sharon Ann Hamilton in the late sixties, but he found little work, got divorced, and dropped out of show business. He traveled around alone, an admitted flower child, obtaining odd jobs until he found his creative outlet in carpentry. He has carved out a satisfying life for himself in the Big Bear Mountains of California. Lee is quoted as saying, "Suddenly after the series was canceled and I began doing guest shots, I realized that something had changed—I wasn't the center of attention anymore. My folks had always told me that my career might not last, but when it happened, it was still a hard thing for me to adjust to."

Jungle Jim

1 Season: 26 half-hour episodes

Network: Syndicated; All episodes black and white

Debut: September 26, 1955 / Finale: March 19, 1956

The title character in *Jungle Jim* was Johnny Weissmuller, previously of 1930s and '40s *Tarzan* movie fame. In this series, Weissmuller, aided by youthful sidekick Skipper and his pet chimp, served as a hunter, guide, and explorer in Africa. Weissmuller was still popular from his movie career, but the poor quality of scripts and filming limited this series to only a single season.

MARTIN HUSTON

(February 8, 1941–August 1, 2001)

Character: Skipper Bradley

"Marty" had a twenty-year career in the business, beginning with guest spots in TV and a starring role in the eleven episode *My Son Jeep*, before he captured a boy's dream-of-a-lifetime role outdoors in the jungle, swinging with a chimp and Johnny Weissmuller. After the series, he continued his fame by nabbing a role in the show *Too Young to Go Steady* followed by *Diagnosis Unknown*. Marty moved to New York, where he lived most of his life enjoying theatrical triumphs. He made his Broadway debut in *Only in America* and created many memorable characters for the stage such as Norman in *Norman, Is That You?* which premiered at the Lyceum Theatre in New York. Martin studied at Columbia University, married, and had three children. He died of cancer at sixty years of age, but having enjoyed his successful transition to an adult actor.

The Mickey Mouse Club

4 Seasons: 332 episodes (length varied; some half-hour, some full-hour)

Network: ABC; All episodes in black and white

Debut: October 3, 1955 / Finale: June 24, 1959

Walt Disney was at the top of his game when *The Mickey Mouse Club* began its daily reign every afternoon on ABC in October 1955. Disneyland was not only the newly opened phenomenal amusement park in Southern California but *Disneyland* was a hit anthology series on ABC that premiered in the fall of 1954 and was hosted by Disney. Everything Walt touched turned to gold in film and animation, and television was no exception. The secret to his success was his ability to connect with children, both the young and the young-at-heart. More importantly, he respected children. *The Mickey Mouse Club* was a popular hangout for kids. It featured a special theme per day of the week and played host to a number of serials for young people. Many of the teen idols of the 1960s were first seen on this very popular show.

The Mickey Mouse Club, c. 1957.

Unknown

SHARON BAIRD

(Born August 16, 1942 [some sources cite 1943])
Character: Sharon

Tap-dancing Sharon was already a professional when she joined the mouse pack. Eddie Cantor was so taken with the little girl that he signed her to a contract to appear monthly on his show and then insured her legs for $50,000. When Cantor had a heart attack in 1952, the whirling Sharon took a rest but then claimed parts in *Death Valley Days* and *The Damon Runyon Theater*. Tapping while twirling a rope and then skipping to it helped her to capture a Mouseketeer role, and she stayed with the show until 1958. Afterward, she performed live at Disneyland, but she did not find many other entertainment jobs. Sharon went to Valley College for two years, worked as a secretary, and married Dalton Lee Thomas in 1964. Although they split two years later, the divorce wasn't final until 1972. In 1969 she started a career as a costumed character working for Sid and Marty Krofft in the TV series *H. R. Pufnstuf*. Her small stature of four feet eight inches made her an ideal candidate to appear in other costumed roles in programs such as *Sigmund and the Sea Monster* and *Lidsville*. Sharon's last acting appearance was in *Mother Goose's Treasury* in 1990. She continues to appear at Mouseketeer reunions and share stories about the mischief of mice.

BOBBY BURGESS

(Born May 19, 1941)
Character: Bobby

Handsome, smiling Bobby had won many amateur dance contests before he won the part of a Mouseketeer. One of the older mice, tall Bobby accomplished many athletic moves in his dance routines, and he often danced with diminutive Sharon and then with Darlene and Doreen. When filming was done for the Club, Bobby went to Long Beach State and continued dancing with his longtime partner, Barbara Boylan. In one of their competitions, at the Aragon Ballroom in Santa Monica in 1961, they won the grand prize: an opportunity to reprise their winning number, "Calcutta," on *The Lawrence Welk Show*. Bobby and Barbara became regulars on the show. After Barbara left, Cissy King became Bobby's partner; Elaine Balden succeeded her. His marriage partner is Kristie Ann Floren, daughter of Welk's accordionist Myron Floren; he married Kristie Ann in 1971, and they have four children. In addition to real estate holdings, Bobby owns Burgess Cotillion in Studio City and continues his love of dance by teaching, traveling, and performing at venues such as Harrah's Lake Tahoe, conventions, and the Lawrence Welk Theater in Branson Missouri. In 2014 he published the book *Ears and Bubbles*. Well, Bobby, we are all ears and attuned to the sparkling bubbles that are still popping in your life as a successful ex–child star.

LONNIE BURR

(Born May 31, 1943)
Character: Lonnie

Smart and talented Lonnie was a confident Mouseketeer. He had several films, TV spots, and acting jobs on radio to his credit before he auditioned for the Club. He also was a trained dancer from the age of four and had been making local live appearances. His personality charmed the producers even though Walt, Lonnie has claimed, could never remember his name. After his stint on the show, he graduated from high school at fifteen and then from UCLA at twenty. He also attained a master's in theatre arts from UCLA. Then he went on to choreograph plays, musicals, live performances, and commercial and industrial shows, and direct TV, radio, and theatre. Lonnie has stayed in touch with his fellow Mouseketeers; he has attended reunions, and he even wrote one of their reunion specials. Lonnie has also written two books, the nonfiction *Two for the Show: Great 20th Century Comedy Teams* (2000) and *Confessions of an Accidental Mouseketeer* (2009), which was updated in 2014 and retitled *The Accidental Mouseketeer*. He has been married since 1970 to Diane Coleridge Dickey, and they live in Maryland. An education and a steady relationship helped Lonnie weather the unsteady waves of the business and guide him to his multiple successes in the various areas of our wonderful world of entertainment.

TOMMY COLE

(Born December 20, 1941)

Character: Tommy

An accordion led the way to Tommy's job as a Mouseketeer. He had been playing in a Western band at local venues, although he did get one gig on TV: *The Ray Bolger Show*. The entire band auditioned for the Club, but he was the only one who was hired. He later declared that he never played the accordion again. After the show, he primarily sang and danced in live performances, and he went on a tour to Australia that Jimmy Dodd had organized for some of the other Mouseketeers. He did a stint in the US Air Force and attended Pasadena City College. On a USO tour in Korea, he met his bride-to-be, Aileen; they married after they returned stateside in the mid '60s. They have two children. Tommy has become an excellent makeup artist; he has been nominated for several Emmy awards for makeup design. He won an Emmy in 1979 for his work on *Backstairs at the White House*. He was elected as the business representative for the Makeup Artists and Hair Stylist Guild, Local 706, which proved to be a full-time job. Embracing the politics of the business he also is the Television Academy Governor of Make Up and Hair and is on the board of directors for the Motion Picture Industry Pension and Health plans. They are all important positions, and Tommy is one important ex–child star!

ANNETTE FUNICELLO

(October 22, 1942–April 8, 2013)
Character: Annette

Brave Annette did not have a hankering to be a Mouseketeer. She was happily dancing and being a model for several stores in the San Fernando Valley in California. But when casting scouts saw her in a school performance of "Ballet vs. Jive," they called her in for an audition. She then took excitedly to her new role as a mouse, but she was more comfortable with the dancing than the singing. After *The Mickey Mouse Club* was canceled, her voice held her in good stead; she recorded such ditties as "Tall Paul," "Oh Dio Mio," and "Pineapple Princess." Annette actually made more money from her recording contract than from her $500-per-week contractual salary from Disney Productions, which had been increased from her original $325 by court order. She appeared in the Disney movies *The Shaggy Dog* and *Babes in Toyland* before she began the Beach Party franchise opposite Frankie Avalon. During that period, she also married Jack Gilardi, and the couple had three children. Annette semiretired from show business to take care of them. She and Jack were divorced in 1981, and Annette married friend and horse trainer Glen Holt in 1986. In 1987, during promotional concerts for *Back to the Beach,* she started experiencing dizzy spells. In 1992 Annette disclosed that she was suffered from multiple sclerosis. During the time of her illness, she dictated her autobiography, *A Dream Is a Wish Your Heart Makes: My Story,* which was published in 1994. After a fire in their Encino home, she and Glen moved to Shaffer, California, where she died from complications of the disease. In 2013 Bob Iger, Chairman of the Walt Disney Company, said, "Annette was and always will be a cherished member of the Disney family, synonymous with the word Mouseketeer and a true Disney Legend." Annette was given the Disney Legend Award and an Angel in Show Business Award. She truly is an angel, still missed and admired by so many of her fans for the remarkable dignity and grace she showed under tragic circumstances.

DARLENE GILLESPIE

(Born April 8, 1941)
Character: Darlene

Branded by some as Disney's "bad seed," talented Darlene, known for her big voice and bigger smile, suffered a tragedy as an ex–child star. She was not afflicted by fire or chronic medical ailments or even narcotic abuse. Hers was a tragedy of the heart and psyche. Darlene was primed to be a star, and Walt Disney and the Mickey Mouse Club were to be her conduits. After the first season of the Club, popular Darlene was cast in one of the fifteen-minute serials attached to the show; it was called *Corky and White Shadow,* a story of a girl and her dog. Playing Corky, Darlene was a hit. She returned to the mischief of mice duties, but the strain of working in the Disney Circus, making appearances, and recording resulted in pneumonia and a six-week recovery period that forced her to forfeit what was to be her next role, in Disney's *Westward Ho, the Wagons,* to Doreen Tracey. And as Darlene's popularity began to slow, Annette's popularity began to grow. A proposed serial, *Annette and Darlene,* was retitled *Annette.* Darlene's contract was not renewed, and she was replaced by Judy Nugent. Darlene was brokenhearted. Decades later, she would sue Disney for what she perceived to be its failure to promote her career as the studio had done for

Annette; after lengthy legal wrangling her suit was finally settled out of court. In 1962, she quit the business altogether; she went on to marry, have two children, divorce, study, and become a nurse. Serious troubles came when she met third husband-to-be Jerry Fraschilla, with whom she embarked on a life of crime in the 1990s. The two were convicted of fraud charges and imprisoned. Darlene was released after eighteen months, but other criminal charges followed her into the twenty-first century. This tragedy of a great talent dismissed by Hollywood and consumed by her own misguided ambitions teaches another lesson about ex–child stars and their fragility.

CUBBY O'BRIEN

(Born July 14, 1946)
Character: Cubby

Carl Patrick O'Brien's mother thought her baby looked like a bear cub and nicknamed him "Cubby." The name stuck. Cubby literally had drumming in his blood. His father was Haskell "Hack" O'Brien, who not only was a professional drummer but also taught the instrument. Cubby started playing the drums at the age of five with gigs on *The Spade Cooley Show* and for live events. He was a natural for the Club, especially after he quickly learned dance routines and how to sing. After the series ended, he segued to *The Lawrence Welk Show* for two years and has been drumming ever since. He married Marilyn Miller, his first wife, in 1966, and they had one child, Alicia. His second marriage lasted twenty-one years. He and his third wife, Holly, live in southwest Washington State, but Cubby still travels to perform with Bernadette Peters or as a drummer in Broadway productions. Responding to a comment in an interview that O' Brien had a relatively smooth introduction to show business, he said, "Child actors are so slick now. We were like the kids next door. If you work with good people and nice people you end up having good experiences, and I've been very lucky." Yes, we'll march to the beat of that drum, Cubby!

KAREN PENDLETON

(Born August 1, 1946)
Character: Karen

Karen became a reluctant post-Mouseketeer. One of the youngest of the mice, she was often paired with Cubby, and they had a good time performing. But when they were offered an extension on their contract, Karen's parents turned it down. Karen left show business, worked as a clerk at the May Company department store, married, had one daughter, Stacy, and divorced. Then tragedy struck, and Karen suffered a near-fatal car accident that left her paralyzed from the waist down. The determination to live her life to the fullest kicked in, and she went to college; she earned a BA at Fresno State and then an MA in psychology and counseling. Karen still lives in Fresno, California; she has worked in women's shelters and at the Center for Independent Living, and she is an advocate for the disabled. She joins some of her fellow Mouseketeers at reunions, and they relive those fun times of being together as a team on one of the most memorable children's variety shows ever.

DOREEN TRACEY

(Born April 13, 1943)
Character: Doreen

Being born into a dancing household helped Doreen hone her craft, and she was selected quickly for a spot on the "Red Team," as Disney production called the first-string Mouseketeers. She was working after school in her parents' LA dance studio and was primed for the audition. I don't know if she was primed for the aftermath of the series ending, however. She sang, danced, and acted through three seasons of the show, and she was especially popular when she joined Jimmy Dodd's tour to Australia. When she returned, Doreen married at the age of eighteen in 1961, had one son, and then divorced in 1962. She toured with the USO during the mid- to late sixties. When she returned, she struggled to live down her Mouseketeer image. "I wanted to identify as an entertainer on my own," she said. "But I couldn't escape my past." She certainly tried by posing nude for the men's magazine *Gallery* in 1976. But she still wore her ears. Disney stopped calling. She tried posing nude again for *Gallery* without the ears but in a trench coat in 1979, outside Disney Studios. It didn't help. She went to work for Frank Zappa in the promotional department and then for Warner Brothers in administration. She has made amends with Disney and occasionally appears with the Mouseketeers, but with her ears off and her trench coat buttoned up.

Fury

5 Seasons: 116 half-hour episodes
Network: NBC; All episodes black and white
Debut: October 15, 1955 / Finale: March 19, 1960

The 1950s was the era in which the Baby Boomers grew up, and they loved shows about animals. And they loved Westerns. The hero in the title role of this series was a beautiful stallion who worked and aided the boys who lived on the Broken Wheel Ranch in California, which gave viewers the best of both worlds. Set in the late fifties, a typical episode revolved around a young guest-star getting into mischief or some kind of trouble. The youth would be rescued by Fury just in time and learn the error of his or her ways. Episodes would sometimes feature youth organizations such as 4-H Club, Junior Achievement, Little League, the Boy Scouts, the Girl Scouts, and others.

Bobby Diamond on the set of *Fury*.

BOBBY DIAMOND

(Born August 23, 1943)

Character: Joey Clark Newton

Bobby was discovered by children's agent Lola Moore when his photo appeared on a magazine cover. He started in "extra" work, and even appeared in Cecil B. DeMille's *The Greatest Show on Earth,* where, during a break, he asked the great director for popcorn. He didn't get the popcorn, but he did continue attaining bit parts before he was cast in the lead in the long-running *Fury.* After the series, he was considered for Don Grady's part in *My Three Sons,* and at the same time, he was offered a regular role in *The Man in the Gray Suit.* According to Bobby, the *Suit* series offered fifty dollars more a week, so he turned down the role in what became a popular sitcom. *Suit* was canceled after one season. Ah, acting decisions! Bobby did nab a recurring role in *The Many Loves of Dobie Gillis* as "Dunky" Gillis, but after that show, it was time for college and gymnastics, in which he won several awards. While seeking a student draft deferment as the war in Vietnam was raging, Bobby became interested in law and subsequently got his law degree at the University of West Los Angeles (at that time called the San Fernando Valley College of Law). Along the way, he reverted to his given name, Robert. He married Tara Parker in 1986, and they had two children, Robert Jr. and Jesse. He is now divorced, practices criminal defense law in Westwood, California, and still wears the smirk that he perfected as a child.

JIMMY BAIRD

(Born November 5, 1945)
Character: Rodney "Pee Wee" Jenkins

Jimmy is the brother of Mouseketeer Sharon. According to Jimmy, whom I saw many times on interviews as a child, we did a commercial together, Sharon had started singing and dancing on *The Colgate Comedy Hour*. Since he admittedly couldn't sing or dance, he took up acting and stayed in the profession from the time he was five until he turned nineteen. Cast as a recurring character on *Fury*, he had parts on many of the TV shows of that time span, including *Have Gun Will Travel* and *My Friend Flicka*. He also acted on radio, and he appeared in approximately twenty-five movies and live TV. At five feet three inches tall, he could always play younger than his years, a plus for a child stars. But his heart really wasn't in acting, and he claims he never took it seriously. Jim went to college and started teaching English in Carpentaria, California, when he was twenty-one. He and his wife still live in that beautiful city. Jim retired in 2007, having enjoyed his life of teaching others what he found so fascinating.

ROGER MOBLEY

(Born January 16, 1949)
Character: "Packy" Lambert

Roger came to the series, his initial foray into television, in its third season. He had sung in the Mobley Trio with his brother and sister at church festivals.

When they appeared on an episode of *Ted Mack and the Original Amateur Hour*, Lola Moore, a children's talent agent, spotted him and signed him. He got his first job on his first interview. After the series ended, Roger continued to act in TV and films. When he was fourteen, Disney cast him in *Emil and the Detectives* and then for the lead in the series *Gallagher*. In 1968 he was drafted, and he trained for the Green Berets. He was sent to Vietnam. Upon his return, he returned to his home state of Texas and married his high school sweetheart, Shari, in 1970. They have three children. He began a career in law enforcement in Texas but moved back to Los Angeles for a relatively brief period to try to resuscitate his career. He got one role in *The Apple Dumpling Gang Rides Again*, but Disney and Hollywood weren't buying anymore. So Roger returned to his Texas police work and took on the job of undercover narcotics agent—one tough cookie! He has also been a wind turbine inspector and is now a pastor at a Bible church in Texas. While watching an episode of *Fury* with his youngest daughter, he commented, "Life can't get any better than that for a kid . . . I spent the summer riding horses and going swimming and got paid for it." Here is one ex–child star who thoroughly enjoyed his childhood acting experiences.

My Friend Flicka

2 Seasons: 39 half-hour episodes

Network: CBS; All episodes were filmed in color but broadcast in black and white originally.

Debut: February 10, 1956 / **Finale:** February 1, 1957

As color television was being developed in the 1950s, executives realized that programs filmed in color would be easier to rerun in syndication later on. But color television was expensive for the industry and the audience of the day; programs aired in color would only be viewed by a small audience. *My Friend Flicka* was filmed in color to make it more attractive to future syndication, but unfortunately, the show only lasted thirty-nine episodes, so it was for naught. Based on both a popular novel and film of the 1940s, like *Fury*, it combined the Western genre with the animal drama, but the cast did not attract the audience. Flicka is a horse who befriends and protects young Ken McLaughlin on a Wyoming ranch, but Flicka did not have the star power of Fury, who was the highest paid "actor" in Hollywood at the time of his eponymous starring role.

Johnny Washbrook.

CBS/Photofest

JOHNNY WASHBROOK

(Born October 16, 1944)
Character: Ken McLaughlin

Johnny began his thirty-five-year acting career with a radio gig at the age of seven in Toronto, Canada. Following in his older brother's acting footsteps, he joined a children's dramatic group and was selected from that group to be in *Peter and the Wolf* for the Canadian Broadcasting Corporation (CBC). Following that and other (minor) roles, he was cast in *My Friend Flicka*. His entire family would need to move from Canada to Los Angeles, which they did gladly. After the series, Johnny worked in the movie *The Space Children* and many of the episodics of the day, including *My Three Sons* and *Hazel*. As an adult, John went to Cal State–Northridge and then traveled to New York, where he worked for twelve years onstage, in movies, and in soap operas. He and his wife, Joy, have one son, Luke. After a trek overseas to study at LAMDA (London Academy of Music And Dramatic Arts) and RADA (Royal Academy of Dramatic Art), he decided on a career change and became a banker—a role he actually played in *A Nightingale Sang in Berkeley Square*. I guess he really liked that part, because he became a senior vice president and loan officer at a small bank in Edgartown, Massachusetts, on Cape Cod. He claims he is enjoying every minute of it!

Circus Boy

2 Seasons: 49 half-hour episodes

Network: NBC 1956–57; ABC 1957–58; All episodes black and white

Debut: September 23, 1956 / Finale: December 12, 1957

What could have been more fun than living at the circus in the late 1800s/early 1900s America as a little boy? Little orphan Corky was lucky enough to go live with his Uncle Joey, a circus clown. Life on the road was exciting for Corky and his pet elephant, Bimbo, as the traveling show encountered new adventures—and some threats—as it moved from town to town every week.

MICKEY DOLENZ (MICKEY BRADDOCK)

(Born March 8, 1945)

Character: Corky

Mickey has maintained a continued presence in show business ever since his start in the *Circus Boy* series, where he was billed as Mickey Braddock. Both his parents were actors. After this series he appeared in episodics, but he primarily concentrated on his studies. When he was chosen as a musician for the Monkees, he did not know how to lift a drumstick—he quickly learned. Since the two-year run of that popular show, which made him a teen idol, he continued with his music career, singing and touring with the group or on his own. He also has appeared on occasional TV episodes of other shows. Mickey has directed stage musicals and appeared in them as well, most notably in *Pippin*. He has been married three times. Evidently he did not have too bad a time as a child star, as he encouraged his daughter Ami in her acting pursuits. He's still acting and touring with the Monkees, with a special tribute to Davy Jones, who died in 2012, incorporated into the act. The beat of this talented ex–child star still goes on.

Bachelor Father

5 Seasons: 157 half-hour episodes
Network: CBS 1957–59; NBC 1959–61; ABC 1961–62; All episodes black and white
Debut: September 15, 1957 / Finale: June 26, 1962

How times have changed! While series have been featuring different types of blended families for a few decades, in 1950s television, it seemed that the vast majority of homes in America had a father and a mother. One exception was *Bachelor Father*, the story of a wealthy playboy and his Asian housekeeper, who find their lives turned upside down when Uncle Bentley's orphaned teenage niece comes to live with them. The suave man-about-town quickly moved his life out of the fast lane to accommodate the charming and lovable waif.

Noreen Corcoran and John Forsythe from *Bachelor Father*.
CBS/Photofest

NOREEN CORCORAN

(October 20, 1943–January 15, 2016)
Character: Kelly Gregg

Already a veteran TV and movie actress, Noreen assumed the role of the niece of wealthy man-about-town John Forsythe after her parents were killed in an automobile accident. Noreen came from a family of actors. Her brother Kevin had starred as Moochie in the Disney series *Spin and Marty,* and her older sister Donna was known for her appearances in *Angels in the Outfield* (1951) and *Don't Bother to Knock.* Ronald Reagan, who was shooting at the same studio where the series was under consideration, recommended Noreen to John Forsythe. And that recommendation held sway. After shooting the series, Noreen appeared in the movie *Gidget Goes to Rome.* An episode of TV's *Big Valley* proved to be her last show business appearance in 1965. She chose to go behind the camera and worked with the Lewitzky Dance Studio. She never married and in 2016 died of cardiopulmonary disease at the age of seventy-two.

JIMMY BOYD

(January 9, 1939–March 7, 2009)
Character: Howard Meechim

He was a fixture in the Hollywood TV scene in the fifties. Gawky, redheaded Jimmy seemed able to fill any teenage role that was needed. Before his recurring role on *Bachelor Father,* Jimmy often appeared on *Date with an Angel* starring Betty White and in a raft of TV commercials. After *Bachelor Father,* he continued to work a lot in TV, most notably in the series *Broadside*. His last appearance in show business was in the movie *Brainstorm*. His origins in the Mississippi backwaters included a grandfather known as "Fiddler Bill," who led Jimmy into music. Jimmy had a nice recording and live performance career and toured the United States with his own comedy and music show when work on TV slowed down. His recording of "I Saw Mommy Kissing Santa Claus" in 1963 sold over two million records in less than ten weeks. He was briefly married to Yvonne Craig, Batgirl in *Batman*. He then married Anne Forrey, and their two-year union produced one child. Prior to his terminal illness, he could be seen sailing in the waters surrounding Marina del Rey, a contented man and ex–child star.

BERNADETTE WITHERS

(Born February 5, 1946)
Character: Ginger Farrell

Bernadette and I were theatrical colleagues; I saw this affable redhead on many interviews in the fifties. Both Bernadette and I appeared early in our careers in the movie *I'll Cry Tomorrow* with Susan Hayward. Bernadette then did many episodics before she landed the role of Ginger on *Bachelor Father*. After the series, she continued in the business, and we appeared together again, in the movie *The Trouble with Angels* starring Rosalind Russell. After that, I went to college, and Bernadette left the scene. She decided "real" business was more for her, and she became a partner in a software company. She lived in Ireland for a while and married twice; each union produced one child. She now lives in Southern California and enjoys reliving her memories as an ex–child star. She claims that *Bachelor Father* was like a real family to her.

The Real McCoys

6 Seasons: 224 half-hour episodes

Network: ABC 1957–62; CBS 1962–63; All episodes black and white

Debut: October 3, 1957 / Finale: June 23, 1963

The Real McCoys was a Danny Thomas/Desilu collaborative effort that one could say was a precursor to *The Beverly Hillbillies*, sans the mansion and millions. The laughs are derived from a mountain family who moves from West Virginia to Southern California to become dirt farmers, and the humor flows from the clash of cultures as the family settles into its new surroundings. Stories would often end with a moral to illustrate how old-time values still hold true in the modern world.

LYDIA REED

(Born August 23, 1944)

Character: Tallahassee "Hassy" McCoy

Hallmark Hall of Fame and *Robert Montgomery Presents* were recipients of Lydia's talents when she was but eight years old. From these TV beginnings, she went on to quality movies such as Bing Crosby's *High Society* and *The Seven Little Foys,* where she played Mary Foy. Lydia was in all five seasons of *The Real McCoys*, but when Kathleen Nolan left in the fourth season due to contract disputes, Lydia as well as Michael Winkelman, who played her younger brother, were used less often in the series. It has been suggested that the growing children were not happy with Kathleen's departure and became more difficult to handle. Lydia made her own departure from show business after the series, except for an appearance in one horror movie. I guess she had had enough drama in her dealings on the real McCoys. Lydia is now living a quiet life with her husband and children in Southern California. She segued from the McCoy farm in San Fernando Valley to a suburban home in San Fernando Valley and discovered the wonders of good health in the process.

MICHAEL WINKELMAN

(June 27, 1946–July 27, 1999)

Character: Little Luke McCoy

Michael and his sister Wendy Winkelman were strong on the interview circuit and on episodic TV during the fifties and early sixties. Michael began his career with appearances in the movie *The Big Knife,* starring Jack Palance, and in the TV series *The Great Gildersleeve.* He played in *The Real McCoys* all five seasons and went on to find work in other episodics. One of his last TV appearances was in *The Munsters.* When work became scarce, he joined the US Navy and was deployed to Vietnam. One of his fellow inductees said that he was a quiet guy in Nam. For a sensitive ex–child star, war was hell. When he returned stateside Michael still found work scarce but did get a job at Universal as a groundskeeper. He unfortunately died at the young age of fifty-three and was laid to rest in Riverside National Cemetery.

Leave It to Beaver

6 Seasons: 234 half-hour episodes and one unaired pilot

Network: CBS 1957–58; ABC 1958–63; All episodes in black and white

Debut: October 4, 1957 / Finale: June 20, 1963

One of the most enduring cultural legacies of 1950s TV is *Leave It to Beaver*. The program has come full circle; it actually seemed more dated when it was viewed in the 1970s and 1980s than it does today. The central story of two brothers making their way into manhood and having each other's backs is more enduring today than ever. Even though Beaver and his brother grew up in the stereotypical nuclear family of the era, so many children today are raised in homes with absentee parents that they learn to rely on one another to learn life's lessons. So whatever the reason, this sweet sitcom remains as relevant today as it did when it first aired—maybe even more so.

Tony Dow and Jerry Mathers from *Leave It to Beaver*.
CBS/ABC/Photofest

JERRY MATHERS

(Born June 2, 1948)

Character: Theodore "Beaver" Cleaver

Parents make all the difference to a child actor, and Jerry was lucky to have an excellent mentor in his mother. He started doing commercials at the tender age of two, and she gently guided him through TV performances and movies before he became the iconic Beaver. After the series ended, Jerry concentrated on academics and graduated from UC–Berkeley with a BS in philosophy. He worked as a bank loan officer and then as a real estate developer. Feeling the theatrical itch, he toured in 1978 in plays and then reprised his role in *Still the Beaver,* which grew to be a syndicated TV series, *The New Leave it to Beaver,* for five years. Twice divorced, he has three children from his second wife, Rhonda Gehring. Diagnosed with Type 2 diabetes, he appears on the lecture circuit for PhRMA (Pharmaceutical Research and Manufacturers of America), and at trade shows, conventions, and on cruise ships to talk about the disease. In 1998 he published his autobiography, *And Jerry Mathers as the Beaver*. Jerry has noted what he considers very important to the mental and physical health of a child star: "My mother and father made sure when we were home, we were part of the family, not a TV star. And the other thing: My father was fully employed while I was doing the series." Very important.

TONY DOW

(Born April 13, 1945)
Character: Wally Cleaver

The producers of *Leave It to Beaver* wanted "real" kids to fill the children's starring roles, and they got them in Jerry and Tony. Tony had almost no previous acting experience, but as a Junior Olympic diving star, he had the confidence to be filmed and also to take on a little brother. His family was supportive, and that attitude helped fuel Tony's creativity throughout his life. After gaining the part of Wally, Tony's attention was on acting, but after the show he expanded his artistic bent. He returned to the syndicated Beaver franchise but began directing some of the episodes. He then went on to producing. In fact, he also produced two children, one with Carol Marlowe and the other with Lauren Shulkind, to whom he is still married. In the 1990s, Tony revealed he suffered from clinical depression, but he has been able to alleviate his condition somewhat and has appeared in self-help videos, including *Beating the Blues*. He now is a recognized sculptor, and his works in burl wood and bronze have been exhibited in the prestigious Société Nationale des Beaux-Arts show at the Louvre. Tony overcame the ex–child star stigma and was able to follow and fulfill his passions.

KEN OSMOND

(Born June 7, 1943)
Character: Eddie Haskell

Eddie Haskell's character was far afield of Ken Osmond's, which is warm and honest, but his excellent portrayal of a bad boy allowed him to keep up a long if not constant presence in the entertainment field. Ken started acting as a child of four and secured the role of Eddie at fourteen. The role was meant for just a one-shot spot, but it lasted through the original series, the TV-movie *Still the Beaver,* and then the new series, *The New Leave It to Beaver.* Ken added other acting roles to his résumé, and then found a second career as an LAPD narcotics and vice motorcycle officer. He has been married since 1969 and has two sons. He has said that his marriage and mortgage on a newly bought home were part of the reasons he took the police job. He now manages rental properties in Los Angeles and makes personal appearances, and he published his memoir, *Eddie: The Life and Times of America's Preeminent Bad Boy,* in 2014. He says he has good memories of his life as a child star, which was filled with unique and special events such as meeting the president of the United States and watching a live space shuttle launch among other experiences that accrue to a well-known young actor.

FRANK BANK

(April 12, 1942–April 13, 2013)
Character: Clarence "Lumpy" Rutherford

Frank appeared in small parts on television before he got the call to audition for the dim-witted but lovable Lumpy. He reprised that role in the TV-movie and second series in the Beaver franchise. But Frank had already left show business when he took on those roles; he had become a successful stock and bond broker, with Jerry Mathers and Barbara Billingsley among his clients. His explicit memoir, *Call Me Lumpy: My* Leave It to Beaver *Days and Other Wild Hollywood Life*, was published in 1997. Frank was married to his third wife, Rebecca, who shared his love of tournament poker, when he passed away at the age of seventy-one, from cancer. I knew him personally as someone who talked like a sailor but had the heart of a saint.

The Donna Reed Show

8 Seasons: 275 half-hour episodes

Network: ABC; All episodes black and white

Debut: September 24, 1958 / Finale: March 19, 1966

Donna Reed set the television standard for the perfect mother and loving, devoted wife who kept house for her doctor husband and two outstanding teenagers. With rarely a hair out of place or without a string of pearls around her neck, Donna faced all of life's challenges with determination and grace. The one time she nearly fell from her lofty perch is when neighbor Dennis the Menace came by to help her paint one afternoon.

Cast photo from *The Donna Reed Show*. Clockwise from left: Shelley Fabares, Donna Reed, Carl Betz, Paul Petersen, Patty Petersen.

SHELLEY FABARES

(Born January 19, 1944)

Character: Mary Stone

Shelley Fabares has enjoyed a long career in show business. From the moment she tapped her way into the theatrical realm at four years old, she applied her talents to create a presence that has withstood the test of Hollywood time. Sharing an interest in acting with her aunt Nanette Fabray and from her start in print modeling to her movie debut in *Letters to Loretta*, both kin have achieved success. After appearing in bit parts in '50s TV shows, Shelley was cast as the big sister to Paul Petersen in the long-running *The Donna Reed Show*. Attaining much success in the popular TV series, Shelly was prompted to leave the show to test her mettle in film. She then appeared only occasionally in the series after 1963. She did find some film fame in three Elvis Presley movies, and her brief foray into the recording world awarded her with a #1 *Billboard* magazine rating. When the series was canceled, she returned full time to doing guest spots on TV shows, peppered with roles in movies. She then lassoed the part of of Brian Keith's daughter in the *The Little People* TV series. After the first year the name was changed to *The Brian Keith Show*, but that did not stop the ratings plunge and the show was canceled. Shelly then grabbed on to another series, *Coach*, which lasted eight years.

After marrying and then divorcing (after a long separation) producer Lou Adler, Shelly married Mike Farrell (*M*A*S*H*). In 2000 Shelly received a liver transplant as a result of an autoimmune disease. She told me this story at the installation of the star for Brian Keith when I commented on her colorful pink, purple, and white punk hair: "I was told that I was dying, and I was lying in my hospital bed. A young woman walked by with purple hair. I thought, I had been so conservative all my life and played so many wholesome parts that I wanted to be free in my last days or months. Dyeing my hair was an outward symbol of what I was feeling."

Shelley recovered, kept her colorful hairdo, and created the voice of Mrs. Kent in the *Superman* TV series and *Justice League*. She now lives a happy and peaceful life watering and planting flowers in the garden of her and Mike's clapboard home, having made a wonderful transition from childhood and teen stardom to a successful adult acting career and all-around good life.

PAUL PETERSEN

(Born September 23, 1945)
Character: Jeff Stone

Paul Petersen not only survived the child actor syndrome but he fought for his peers in the entertainment world. After his successful run in *The Donna Reed Show*, he pursued a brief singing career and became a teen heartthrob. His renditions of "Lollipops and Roses" and "She Can't Find Her Keys" (a subject true to this day!) were top-ten hits. Further roles in movies such as *The Happiest Millionaire* and *Journey to Shiloh* followed before he found his career and personal life breaking up. Married briefly to Brenda Benet, he lost her to Bill Bixby. He went to college, earned a degree in English, and wrote sixteen adventure-oriented fiction books while also running a limousine service. His true passion came to light after the death of Rusty Hamer. He felt moved to help child actors deal with the difficult transition from child acting to adult life and established A Minor Consideration, a nonprofit organization whose mission is to help them do so. Paul has been quite successful in advocating for legal protection for child actors. He is presently married to his third wife, the former Rana Platz, a studio nurse. From his second wife, Hallie Litman, he has two children, one of whom is a casting director. Many ex–child stars owe their present psychological health to Paul's hard work and his fight for the financial and physical rights of those under eighteen in the labor markets. His legacy will long remain.

PATTY PETERSEN

(Born December 2, 1954)
Character: Trisha Stone

Sometimes nepotism pays off. Patty became the younger adopted sister on *The Donna Reed Show*; she was Paul Petersen's real sister. Her time in show business was short, however. When the series ended in 1966 after Patty's three-year stint, she appeared in a few commercials and some industrials and then retired. She became a songwriter and then married and had two children. Presently Patty Petersen Mirkovich owns an Internet company that helps new authors get published, and she is a contributor in part to the Donna Reed Foundation. Sometimes acting isn't for everyone, even if your brother was a teen idol.

The Rifleman

5 Seasons: 168 half-hour episodes

Network: ABC; All episodes black and white

Debut: September 30, 1958 / Finale: April 8, 1963

Another of the dozens of Westerns that populated the landscape of 1950s TV, *The Rifleman* stood out because of the chemistry between series star Chuck Connors and Johnny Crawford, who played the widowed rancher's young son. Casting was the key; had anyone else played the lead characters, the stories would have turned out corny, syrupy, and unbelievable. Connors and Crawford, however, made viewers believe that "each other" was all these two denizens of the Old West had in their rough new world, and they conveyed the love, respect, and devotion that must have been required of families in those harsher times.

Chuck Connors as Lucas McCain and Johnny Crawford as his son, Mark, from the television program *The Rifleman*, 1960.

ABC

JOHNNY CRAWFORD

(Born March 26, 1946)
Character: Mark McCain

Like many child actors who achieved long-lasting fame by lassoing a starring part in a series, Emmy-nominated Johnny had trod the boards for many TV shows and was even a dancing Mouseketeer for half a season. After *The Rifleman*, he acted in more episodics, but he eventually followed his musical heart and created a dance orchestra. Johnny travels and leads the group, which plays classic and vintage music to the great delight of his audiences. He also has recorded CDs to go along with this endeavor. I acted with Johnny on an episode of *The Rifleman* as a teenager and found him to be very personable. Fast-forward to MeTV, where we cohosted a marathon, and he was just as personable. Some child stars can make the adjustment.

Dennis the Menace

4 Seasons: 146 half-hour episodes

Network: CBS; All episodes black and white

Debut: October 4, 1959 / Finale: July 7, 1963

Dennis the Menace endures today due mainly to the talents of star Jay North, who could interact with the citizens of his nameless Midwestern town with mischief but without being annoying or unbelievable. Dennis was a menace not because he wished to cause trouble, but rather because his boyish energy and enthusiasm to be helpful would often lead to disaster. Most often the object of his "help" was his retired next-door neighbor, the hapless and exasperated Mr. Wilson.

The cast of *Dennis the Menace*. Clockwise from center: Jay North, Herbert Anderson, Gloria Henry, Sylvia Field, Joseph Kearns, 1960.

JAY NORTH

(Born August 3, 1951)
Character: Dennis Mitchell

The enigma of child stars and actors in general is that many times they get a role based on their talent and sensitivity; then that very sensitivity provides fodder for their emotional crises. Jay started acting in small jobs helped by his his mother, who worked at AFTRA, the American Federation of Television and Radio Artists. He was seen at a local show by my former agent Hazel McMillan, who signed him, booked him on some episodics, and helped him get the job on *Dennis the Menace*. When the series ended, Jay was tired, but he found work again in the movies *Zebra in the Kitchen* and *Maya,* and the latter's subsequent, short-lived TV series. Then the teenage years hit him hard. He alleges emotional abuse at the hand of his aunt and her husband, who served as his guardians when he worked on set. Wondering what to do next, he joined the navy, but he had no love for swabbing decks and he got an early out. While he tried to find more acting jobs, he couldn't shake the image of the adorable little boy with the platinum-blond hair. He met his third wife (his first two marriages were very short-lived), moved to Florida, and now works as a correctional officer there. Jay has said, "I'm going to write my autobiography; then I'm just going to live a contented, happy life here in Lake Butler with the people I love and kind of just vanish into the mists."

JEANNIE RUSSELL

(Born October 22, 1950)

Character: Margaret Wade

Jeannie came from a musical family. Her mother was a dancer and concert pianist; her father was a backup singer for Mae West who also performed briefly with the Lettermen. When Dad encountered a colleague whose husband was a theatrical agent, he immediately sang the praises of his adorable children. Jeannie and her brother were signed and began their theatrical careers. Jeannie started working in episodics before she captured the iconic role of Margaret in the series. Jeanne (who dropped the *i* of her onscreen name) has said that she has wonderful memories of her time on the show and with her relationship with Jay. She remarked, "It was a very well-written show, and we had a great cast." Following *Dennis,* she appeared in other TV series, such as *Death Valley Days* and *The Deputy,* and in Alfred Hitchcock's movie *The Birds.* She wrapped up her acting career at fifteen—with a commercial. Jeanne proceeded to chiropractic school in Los Angeles and has been counseling people on good health and good posture ever since. No more slices of Mrs. Wilson's pies for her!

THE 1960s

My Three Sons

12 Seasons: 380 half-hour episodes

Network: ABC (1960–65) black and white; CBS (1965–72) in color

Debut: September 29, 1960 / Finale: April 13, 1972

Producer Don Fedderson changed the landscape of television when he created *My Three Sons*. While the popularity of Lucy Ricardo's adventures in Hollywood in the mid-1950s episodes of *I Love Lucy* made it fashionable for movie stars to make guest appearances and cameos on TV, it was still unthinkable to lure a movie star to headline a weekly series—until *My Three Sons*.

Fedderson knew the issue for movie stars appearing on television was no longer one of class conflict (in the early years of TV, it was seen as beneath a movie star's dignity to appear on the small screen); it was about a conflict of time. When Fedderson approached the popular Fred MacMurray about helming *My Three Sons*, MacMurray wanted to do it, but he didn't think the weekly grind of a television series (at a time when a typical season produced thirty-nine episodes compared to today's average of twenty-two) would allow him to maintain his other business, personal, and acting commitments.

Shown from left: Stanley Livingston, Barry Livingston, Don Grady, and Fred MacMurray on the set of *My Three Sons*. *CBS/Photofest*

So Fedderson solved the time problem with what is now commonly known as the Fedderson Method, which goes something like this: All the scripts for a season are prepared in advance for that season, then the scenes with the star are filmed over a thirty-day period (out of sequence). The remaining cast works for several months filming the shots that do not include the star, who then returns for a second round of filming for thirty days to finish his or her part of the season. It worked so well that *My Three Sons* ran successfully for twelve seasons, and Fedderson was even able to export it to another popular show, Brian Keith's *Family Affair*!

My Three Sons began with the simple plot device of an all-male household headed by a widower, with his father-in-law, and the three boys. By its final season, the cast had expanded widely, all the adult sons as well as MacMurray's character were married, and the show focused more on the daily life of an extended, nontraditional family.

TIM CONSIDINE

(Born December 31, 1940)
Character: Mike Douglas

Emanating from a show business family—his maternal grandfather was Alexander Pantages of the eponymous theatre—Tim already had movie (*The Shaggy Dog*) and TV (*Spin and Marty*) credits under his theatrical belt before he debuted in Fedderson's *My Three Sons* series in 1960. He appeared in additional acting roles after he left the show to then pursue his true passion of motor sports. Tim has authored books on the subject such as *The Language of Sport* and *American Grand Prix Racing*. Being written out of the show enabled Tim to write his own life story.

DON GRADY

(June 8, 1944–June 27, 2012)
Character: Robbie Douglas

Don got a leg up on the entertainment industry when his mother became a theatrical agent specializing in child actors. Mary Grady was a respected representative for many budding talents, and she helped Don secure parts with Disney and other top producers. After his twelve-year acting stint on *My Three Sons*, Don pursued another passion, which was music. He enjoyed a successful second career as a composer for the movie *Switch,* a stage musical called *EFX*, and other works. But Don also starred as an actor in musicals such as *Pippin* and *Godspell.* He married Ginny Lewsader in 1985, and they had two children, Tessa, who is an actress, and Joey. Don continued his successful show business career until he died of cancer in 2012.

STANLEY LIVINGSTON

(Born November 24, 1950)

Character: Richard "Chip" Douglas

Stanley Livingston was the youngest boy in the *My Three Sons* trifecta until eldest brother, Tim Considine (Mike), left the show due to contractual differences. Stan's real-life brother Barry Livingston (Ernie) was adopted by the Douglas family, and Stan moved up to middle child status. Don Grady (Robbie) started dating Tina Cole (Katie Miller) as he assumed number-one position in the household. Stan later became a producer, director, and editor. He is also a skilled and well-respected artisan who creates beautiful stained-glass objets d'art that depict abstractions, landscapes, and celebrities such as Marilyn Monroe, Lucille Ball, and even the three brothers of *My Three Sons* in beautiful sparkling panes of shimmering glass. He was married to Sandra Goble from 1968 to 1974, and they had one daughter, Samantha. Stan is presently promoting his *The Actors Journey for Kids* DVDs and workshops to illustrate how child acting in the entertainment world can be done right.

BARRY LIVINGSTON

(Born December 17, 1953)

Character: Ernie Thompson Douglas

A stable family life and later a good marriage with his wife, Karen, in 1983 helped Barry make the transition from child to adult actor. Barry assumed the role of Ernie after the first two years of *My Three Sons*. He had previously worked on *The*

Adventures of Ozzie and Harriet, The Dick Van Dyke Show, and *The Lucy Show*. He embraced the world of acting and remained with *My Three Sons* until its end in 1972. Barry continues to act; he played David Marmor in the Academy Award–winning film *Argo* and has frequent guest-star roles on TV such as in *Two and a Half Men* and *Anger Management*. His autobiography, *The Importance of Being Ernie: From My Three Sons to Mad Men, a Hollywood Survivor Tells All,* has received excellent reviews and is filled with interesting anecdotes and truisms. Barry is a child star who has enjoyed his former status and is able to enjoy his present success as a sought-after actor, faithful husband , and devoted father to his two children.

DAWN LYN

(Born January 11, 1963)
Character: Dodie Douglas

The youngest actor to work on *My Three Sons*, Dawn Lyn joined the successful series when she was a mere six years old. When the show ended three years later, Dawn continued to work steadily in film and TV. Finding roles diminishing as she reached adulthood but not great physical height—she is four feet ten inches tall—Dawn began using her voice to her advantage. She still records for the Avalon Community Radio Troupe on Santa Catalina Island in California. One of Dawn's final roles as a child star was on the third season premiere of *Wonder Woman*, where she costarred with her infamous teen idol brother, Leif Garrett. Leif had his problems with childhood and teen stardom. Just before his eighteenth birthday, he crashed his Porsche while under the influence and left his good friend a paraplegic. He continued to have issues with drug addiction, but he finally reemerged after rehab, sober and feeling as though the fog had lifted. He was quoted as saying, "When you've got that sort of power at that young age, and everything at your doorstep, you put out that boy image." Leif was branded as the "bad boy," but that reputation has faded. He now has a clearer vision and his sister Dawn for emotional support.

The Andy Griffith Show

8 Seasons: 249 half-hour episodes

Network: CBS; 1960–65, black and white; 1965–68, color

Debut: October 3, 1960 / Finale: April 1, 1968

Few people know that this long-running and very popular series began as a spin-off of an episode of *The Danny Thomas Show* in 1960. Danny Williams refused to pay a speeding ticket issued by small-town sheriff Andy Taylor, and a new star was born! Griffith once said he attributed the success, quality, and freshness of his series to the fact that the comedy did not tell jokes; its humor was all derived from simple human interactions and characters. Many could relate to the citizens of Mayberry enduring a loved one's rancid homemade pickles so as not to hurt her feelings or accepting the shortcomings of a best friend who spread embarrassing gossip that went awry in a small town. Viewers enjoyed tender moments of learning between a father and son, such as when a bird was accidentally killed by a wayward slingshot missile. Everyday folks: That was the secret to *The Andy Griffith Show*.

Cast photo from *The Andy Griffith Show*. From left: Andy Griffith, Ron Howard, Don Knotts, Jim Nabors.

CBS/Photofest

RONNY HOWARD

(Born March 1, 1954)
Character: Opie Taylor

This is one of the big ex–child star success stories. Not succumbing to drugs, typecasting, or cynicism, the adult Ron was able to forge a successful career as a writer, director, producer, and loving father and husband. His success can be attributed to a stable family background as well as his own motivation and drive to create the best. Ron came from a showbiz family; his father, Rance, who attended drama school at Oklahoma University, was featured in plays, films, and on TV as Howard Broomhauer in the series *Gentle Ben,* which also starred his younger son, Clint Howard. Acting genes certainly were passed on to Ron. After his initial work on *The Andy Griffith Show*, Ron enjoyed fame as an actor in *Happy Days* and then became a respected director and producer in film and television. Some of his award-winning movies include *Apollo 13, Backdraft, EDtv,* and *Parenthood,* for which I, Kathy, your humble author, worked under Ron's direction in postproduction as part of the loop group. His 2002 film *A Beautiful Mind* received an Oscar for his direction and production. Ron produced the TV series *Arrested Development* (which has been revived on Netflix and is expected to get a fifth season); he has also narrated and appeared on the show at times. There's a bit of irony here: This talented adult is a great example of how early childhood stardom doesn't necessarily lead to arrested development in real life.

Hazel

5 Seasons: 154 half-hour episodes

Network: NBC (1961–65); CBS (1965–66); Season 1, black and white except for one
   color episode; remaining seasons, color

Debut: September 28, 1961 / Finale: April 11, 1966

Hazel, based on Ted Key's single-panel comic strip, was a clever domestic sitcom
that pitted an upscale wealthy lawyer against his live-in domestic engineer (Hazel),
whom he couldn't fire because she practically raised his wife when she was a child.
Series star Shirley Booth was at the top of her game as the Emmy-winning title
character, after achieving success and receiving an Oscar, a Tony, and a Golden
Globe for her work onstage and in film. The formula for *Hazel* was familiar but
successful: Her boss finds himself in a bind in business or with finances and ignores
Hazel's commonsense advice, only to realize later that she had the solution to his
problem the whole time.

BOBBY BUNTROCK

(August 4, 1952–April 7, 1974)

Character: Harold "Sport" Baxter

Bobby's theatrical career was tragically cut short when he was twenty-one. He had entered show business at the age of seven and was doing guest spots on TV shows such as *Wagon Train* and *Mr. Ed* before he was cast as the adorable child of Don DeFore and Whitney Blake in 1961. After four years his faux parents left the show but Bobby continued on and inherited a sibling, played by Julia Benjamin (who also had a guest spot on *Family Affair*) and two guardians: Lynn Borden (who also appeared on *Family Affair*) and Ray Fulmer. Bobby was killed in 1974 in a car accident on the same bridge in South Dakota where his mother had died one year previous.

JULIA BENJAMIN

(Born February 21, 1957)

Character: Cousin Susie Baxter

Julia, daughter of successful casting director Phil Benjamin, found herself able to prove her worth even in the nepotistic entertainment world. After her successful five-year stint in the series, Julia appeared in *The Rockford Files* and other TV shows. She then traveled to New York and found a nice career in the voice-over and commercial realm. She suffered a traumatic event when she was mauled by a hundred-pound Akita, but she recovered and stabilized her life. Besides working as an actress, Julia spends time as an advocate for child actors.

The Dick Van Dyke Show

5 Seasons: 158 half-hour episodes plus one hour-long special in 2004
Network: CBS; All 1960s episodes, black and white; 2004 special, color
Debut: October 3, 1961 / Finale: June 1, 1966 (May 11, 2004)

Considered one of the classic sitcoms of television history, *The Dick Van Dyke Show* followed the work and home life of comedy writer Rob Petrie (Van Dyke). It also launched the career of Mary Tyler Moore, who played his wife, whose own successful series in the 1970s led to many popular spin-offs. *The Dick Van Dyke Show* was a domestic comedy with intelligence; in other words, there were no wacky schemes, dizzy wives, dumb husbands, or troublemaking children. Like *The Andy Griffith Show*, *The Dick Van Dyke Show* mined its humor from everyday situations that viewers could identify with.

The Petrie family from *The Dick Van Dyke Show*. From left: Mary Tyler Moore, Dick Van Dyke, Larry Matthews, 1963.
CBS

LARRY MATHEWS

(Born August 15, 1955)

Character: Ritchie Petrie

Larry had a short but important career as the son of Rob and Laura Petrie. As the adorable and witty Ritchie, Larry was able to trade quips with his formidable costars and have fun on the show. When the series ended, he decided that the acting world was not for him, although he did appear in a handful of shows, including documentaries on child stars. He graduated from UCLA and became a successful account executive. He returns to the entertainment realm occasionally to get a stimulating dose of past fame at autograph conventions and in TV interviews such as *Entertainment Tonight*. Although he is in the conservative business world, you know it is that same personable and fun-filled Larry/Ritchie when you see him at celebrity shows with his nails painted a distinctive satiny black color.

The Lucy Show

6 Seasons: 156 half-hour episodes

Network: CBS; 1962–63, black and white; 1963–68, color (but broadcast in black and white through 1965 for cost-effectiveness)

Debut: October 1, 1962 / **Finale:** March 11, 1968

Lucille Ball made her triumphant return to weekly television two years after America's heart was broken by her divorce from husband Desi Arnaz, her *I Love Lucy* costar. Produced by Arnaz in its first season, Ball convinced Vivian Vance, her costar and partner-in-crime from her previous *Lucy* shows, to join her on *The Lucy Show*. Ball portrayed a widow with two children who shared her home with divorced best friend Vivian and her son to make ends meet. Stories were reminiscent of the earlier Lucy era, and ratings soared. Arnaz exited after the first season, and Vance followed after the third season, which led to many format and cast changes. What began as a suburban East Coast domestic comedy in 1962 with two single mothers and their children wound up as a West Coast sitcom about a widowed secretary working for the harried trustee of her late husband's estate. Ball ended the show in 1968 after selling Desilu to Gulf & Western; she returned later that year with *Here's Lucy*. More on that later!

CANDY MOORE

(Born August 26, 1947)
Character: Chris Carmichael

Candy, like many child actors, gained credits appearing in episodic TV shows before getting her own sitcom. After stints on *Leave It to Beaver* and *Rawhide,* she gained the honor of being cast as the daughter of Lucille Ball. Her character lasted for three seasons before the premise and cast were changed. Candy continued as an actor until 1982, essaying such roles as Bebe in *The Donna Reed Show* as the girlfriend of Paul Petersen and as Linda in *Raging Bull*. She then retired from acting and became an author and journalist. Candy is now a teacher in the East Los Angeles Performing Arts Academy Magnet at Esteban E. Torres High School, sharing insights and experience gleaned from her early entry into the business world.

JIMMY GARRETT

(Born September 23, 1954)
Character: Jerry Carmichael

Jimmy was a "baby-actor"; he made his first appearance at the age of nine months in a film and his first commercial at two years. Prior to *Lucy* he appeared in episodic TV including the shows *Twilight Zone* and *Playhouse 90*. During his *Lucy* days, the boy with the sharp wit also appeared in the movie *Munster, Go Home*. When *Lucy* ended, Jimmy quit acting but stayed in show business by working as a talent agent and then went into television production. As a production accountant and financial and/or production coordinator, he has been involved in such shows as *Chicago Hope*, *Martial Law*, and *Celebrity Boxing*. Lately, Jimmy has worked for Smith and Weed on their projects for sports and game shows. He was able to adjust to life after *Lucy* very well. In 2015 he was presented with the Lifetime Achievement Award by the Southern California Motion Picture Council for his contributions to the entertainment world and especially to the beloved *Lucy*.

RALPH HART

(Born May 27, 1952)
Character: Sherman Bagley

As Vivian Vance's son, Ralph was ten years old when he began the series and previously had acted in a few small parts in film. But when Vivian decided to leave the show and the producers decided she should take her son with her, Ralph decided that he would pack up his showbiz bags altogether. His last role was as Kerwin in two epsiodes of *My Three Sons*. Ralph has only attended one Lucy Comedy Fest, which is held every August in Jamestown, and that was because a band of fans had scouted him out. He relented to their appeals and appeared on a panel at the festival in 2008. Ralph is now a hydrogeologist in California. It seems when he makes up his mind to do something—like quit showbiz—he is rock solid in his decision!

The Patty Duke Show

3 Seasons: 104 half-hour episodes and one pilot episode
Network: ABC; All episodes black and white
Debut: September 18, 1963 / Finale: April 27, 1966

Despite achieving an Academy Award at a very young age for her challenging role in *The Miracle Worker*, Patty Duke's greatest acting challenge was her dual role and grueling schedule on the domestic sitcom *The Patty Duke Show*. Geared toward "'tween" and teen audiences, Duke convincingly portrayed twin cousins Patty Lane and Cathy Lane in over 104 episodes in just three years (and she portrayed a third cousin from the South in one episode!). While the stories involved Patty behaving irresponsibly—forgettable foibles—and the more sensible Cathy bailing her out, the show still entertains when you remember that one young actress is playing both roles. A 1999 reunion movie, *Still Rockin' in Brooklyn Heights*, presented the cast in an entertaining, modern, grown-up version of the original series. And we finally got to see Patty and Cathy in color!

Patty Duke.
ABC/Photofest

PATTY DUKE

(Born December 14, 1946)

Character: Patty Lane/Cathy Lane

My friend Patty, born Anna Marie Duke, is a prime example of child-actor abuse, success, and survival. In her book *Just Call Me Anna*, Patty chronicled her mistreatment by childhood managers, her bipolar condition, and her eventual breakthrough to a full understanding of herself through friendship, therapy, and good relationships. Her second book, *A Brilliant Madness,* is a bestseller and further tells the tale of her mental issue. At the beginning of her career, Patty was hired by advertisers to do commercials through her managers, the Rosses. She then grabbed the starring role of Helen Keller in *The Miracle Worker* on Broadway. She went on to reprise her role in film and received the accolade of Best Supporting Actress from the Academy. Then writer-producer Sidney Sheldon devised *The Patty Duke Show* for her, and shortly thereafter, she married Harry Falk, thirteen years her senior.

The show and her marriage to Falk ended. She tried to change her image and starred in *The Valley of the Dolls.* The film became a cult favorite, but it didn't change her image. That happened when she appeared in the TV-movie *My Sweet Charlie* and won the Emmy for Outstanding Lead Actress in a miniseries or movie. After that, audiences accepted her as more than just the young characters she had previously played, and she starred in many TV-movies and films. She came to realize that she had bipolar disorder, which used to be called manic depression. Pre-diagnosis, Patty had tried alcohol and drugs to appease her mental monster. When the disease was correctly diagnosed, she started taking lithium and other medication to put her on a more even keel. She has been able to continue in her award-winning roles, find happiness with her husband, Michael Pearce, and enjoy the beauty of where they live in Idaho. Patty and Michael have an adopted son, Kevin. Patty has two other children: Sean Astin (whose father is Michael Tell) and Mackenzie Astin. She is enjoying the fruits of her successful transition from child acting, her hard work, her wonderful awards, and most importantly her grandchildren.

EDDIE APPLEGATE

(Born October 4, 1935)
Character: Richard Harrison

Eddie Applegate, the second banana to Patty on the show, is still friends with his costar. He started his career on episodic TV with such shows as *The Many Loves of Dobie Gillis* and *Mr. Novak* until he landed the role of Patty's boyfriend. After the series he continued his acting career, popping up on parts in movies and TV shows such as *Daktari*, *Gunsmoke*, and *Nancy*. He rejoined Patty on a TV-movie in 1999 and played the grown-up version of himself on *The Patty Duke Show: Still Rockin' in Brooklyn Heights*. Eddie is still acting, appearing in the movie *Rain from Stars* released in 2013. Over the years, he worked on his art and painting during dry spells from acting. He is a former vice president and remains a member of the San Fernando Valley Art Club. Betty Jenkins is his longtime wife, and they live in Chatsworth, California, enjoying the sunshine and basking in the light of a memorable career.

The Farmer's Daughter

3 Seasons: 101 half-hour episodes

Network: ABC; 1963–65. black and white; 1965–66, color

Debut: September 20, 1963 / Finale: April 22, 1966

Based on the successful Loretta Young film of the same name in 1947, this updated version of the story starred beautiful Inger Stevens in the title role as governess to the children of a widowed congressman (William Windom). The series followed the unfolding love story of the leads while Inger cared for the politico's children and elderly mother. The couple married in the third season and quietly closed shop in the spring of 1966.

MICKEY SHOLDAR

(Born March 20, 1949)

Character: Steven Morley

Mickey had a brief but interesting career. He began on TV in other sitcoms such as *The Ann Southern Show* and *Dennis the Menauce*. At thirteen, when he was cast in *The Farmer's Daughter*, he was just starting into his teens and has stated that he did a lot of growing up on the show and that "everybody treated him very well." The producers tried to promote him as a singer, and in one episode the character Steven put together a band called Moe Hill and the Mountain, which included Davy Jones in his pre-Monkees days. Keith Thibodeaux played the drummer—a pre–child star reunion. After his regular role on *The Farmer's Daughter*, Mickey made several appearances in *Dragnet 1967*. His last appearance in front of a camera was in 1974, as a golf pro in the TV-movie *Babe* (about Babe Didrikson). I guess golf was more appealing than acting as he went on to other pursuits. He was married to Janet Lee Hartel from 1974 until 1979, and they had one child.

RORY O'BRIEN

(Born April 19, 1955)

Character: Danny Morley

As the younger brother, Rory's character got away with a lot. Before the show, Danny had gained acting experience in such TV episodics as *Dr. Kildare*, *Bonanza*, and *The Twilight Zone*. He was able to sustain his career for a few years after the series ended, appearing in such fare as *Barnaby Jones* and *The Murdering Class*, with a small part in the highly acclaimed 1970 film *Little Big Man*. In the '70s, however, Rory had had his fill. He slowly slipped out of show business and is now living a quiet life away from the bright lights and past childhood stardom. His part in the movie *Little Big Man* as the assassin must have killed his career.

Petticoat Junction

7 Seasons: 222 half-hour episodes
Network: CBS; 1963–65, black and white; 1965–70, color
Debut: September 24, 1963 / Finale: April 4, 1970

The second of three super-successful '60s sitcoms by producer Paul Henning, *Petticoat Junction* spun Bea Benaderet off from *The Beverly Hillbillies* after that show's first hit season. Benaderet played a different character here; she became Widow Kate Bradley, who struggled to stay afloat financially with her old-country hotel, older countrified Uncle Joe, and three beautiful young daughters. Set in quaint state-less Hooterville, USA, the program was an immediate hit and spun off a third program, *Green Acres*, two years later. All three programs crossed over several times over the years, and while Kate often succeeded in fending off the efforts of the miserly Homer Bledsoe in his drive to shut down the Hooterville Cannonball, the Valley's main form of transportation, Bea couldn't beat cancer. The show continued after her death in 1968 with June Lockhart in a similar role, but Benaderet was the indispensable glue to the show, and the hotel closed for good in 1970.

Cast photo from *Petticoat Junction*. From left: Pat Woodell, Linda Kaye Henning, Jeannine Riley.

CBS/Photofest

LINDA KAYE HENNING

(Born September 16, 1944)
Character: Betty Jo Bradley

My friend Linda Kaye came from a showbiz family; her father was the famous writer/producer of such sitcoms as *The Beverly Hillbillies, Green Acres*, and yes, *Petticoat Junction*. Linda Kaye was the only one of the original three daughters to remain with the show the entire seven seasons. Mike Minor, the oldest son of the producer of *Family Affair,* became Linda's reel husband on *Petticoat*. The "incestuous" nature of the business again took over when she married him in real life. Linda appeared on *Family Affair* and other episodics, divorced, remarried, and now works at a boutique store in North Hollywood close to her home. Linda enjoys filling the rest of her time as a docent at the Los Angeles Zoo, where she shares her experience and love of animals. Linda and I experienced great times when we toured with the play *Vanities,* which was produced by James Doolittle and me in the 1980s. Linda Kaye has told me she enjoyed her acting career. It seems that living in a showbiz world didn't hurt her one bit.

PAT WOODELL

(July 12, 1944–September 29, 2015)
Character: Bobbie Jo Bradley

Pat was the original Bobbie Jo Bradley, but she only stayed with the series for two seasons. She made her acting debut in an episode of *Cheyenne* in 1962 and quickly was cast in other episodics. Although she enjoyed acting in the series, like many young women with stars in their eyes, Pat thought she could fulfill her real passion, which was singing and film stardom, so she quit the popular bucolic TV series. After a few TV guest star roles, an appearance as a singer on *The Hollywood Palace,* four films, and a singing tour with Jack Benny, the stars in her eyes dimmed and she left show business in 1973. She went to work for Werner Erhard, founder of EST (Erhard Seminar Training), which encouraged people to be themselves rather the playing an imposed role. She later cofounded a consulting firm, which she ran unitl 2013, and then retired. Pat passed away at her home in Fallbrook, California, of cancer, which she had battled for more than twenty years.

LORI SAUNDERS

(Born October 4, 1941)
Character: Bobbie Jo Bradley II

Lovely Lori Saunders had a longer duration on *Petticoat* than Pat Woodell, starting her stint in 1965 and staying with the show until its end. She has enjoyed a creative career as actress, photographer, and sculptor. Beginning her career in the classic *Ozzie and Harriet* series in 1952, Lori found iconic status in the countrified series; she changed her given name of Linda to Lori (Saunders was also a screen name) so she would not be confused with Linda Henning. Moving on to other rural programming when *Petticoat* ended in 1970, Lori appeared in *The Beverly Hillbillies* as Betty Gordon, Mr. Drysdale's secretary, in the last season of that series.

Lori continued her bucolic parts when she starred in the one-season series *Dusty's Trail,* which also starred Bob Denver (*Gilligan's Island* graduate) and Forrest

Tucker (*F Troop* senior). Lori's husband, Bernard Sandler, who owned a theatrical agency, may have been instrumental in trying to change her innocent image into a more edgy persona. She embraced slasher films in the '80s, but her innocent image was too difficult to alter, and Lori retired from the business after her last film, *Captive,* which starred David Ladd and Cameron Mitchell. She now resides in Montecito with Bernard and happily creates art and devotes time to charitable organizations and her two grandchildren.

JEANNINE RILEY

(Born October 1, 1940)

Character: Billie Jo Bradley I

Like her costar Pat Woodell, Jeannine also had visions of singing and film stardom. She started her career with an uncredited part in the movie *Five Finger Exercise* in 1962. TV shows in which she was cast included *Route 66* and *My Three Sons*. She was on a roll. Jeannine then captured the original role of Billie Jo, but like Pat, Jeannine only stayed with the show for two seasons, from 1963 to 1965. She was tapped for other roles in TV episodics *Occasional Wife* and *The Smothers Brothers Show*, but her country appeal was too strong, so parts in *The Wild Wild West* and the unsold pilot of *Lil' Abner* were destined for her résumé. The Madera-born Californian couldn't escape her country persona, and after appearances on *Hee Haw* and a stint on *Dusty's Trail* with her other costar, Lori Saunders, she hit the road for non–show-business endeavors. Her last film appearance was in 1991, when she played a landlady in *Timebomb,* starring Robert Culp and Tracy Scoggins. She was married to and divorced from Gary Groom.

GUNILLA HUTTON

(Born May 15, 1944)
Character: Billie Jo Bradley II

Most notable for her one-year stint as the second Billie Jo on *Petticoat Junction*,
Swedish-born Hutton found more success as a regular on *Hee Haw* up to 1992.
Cast as a model in a *Perry Mason* episode in 1965, the beautiful Gunilla appeared in
other TV shows after *Petticoat* such as *Love, American Style* and *Swim Team*. While
appearing on *Hee Haw*, she released several singles and appeared on programs such as
a *Fantasy Island* and *The Love Boat* and the game shows *The Match Game* and *Password*.
In her autobiography, Natalie Cole claimed that Gunilla was the longtime mistress
to her father, Nat King Cole. Gunilla has one child, Amber.

MEREDITH MACRAE

(May 30, 1944–July 14, 2000)
Character: Billie Jo Bradley III

Emanating from a show business family—her parents were the handsome leading
man Gordon MacRae and actress Sheila MacRae—Meredith was destined for
a considerable time span in the industry. She won the role of Billie Jo in 1966,
replacing Gunilla Hutton, after having appeared in such fare as *My Three Sons*. She
joined the girls in the Hooterville singing trio as her genes dictated and recorded
two songs, but acting was more her forte. I replaced Meredith for a time as host of
Mid-Morning L.A. when she sailed off to cruise the seas. Meredith and I had also

been at UCLA at the same time, but she was a Tri Delta and I was a Pi Beta Phi, and our academic paths never crossed. She contracted brain cancer, but her allergic reaction to a medication she took to alleviate her condition caused her cerebellum to swell and was the ultimate cause of her early demise.

Bewitched

8 Seasons: 254 half-hour episodes

Network: ABC; 1964–66, black and white; 1966–72, color

Debut: September 17, 1964 / Finale: March 25, 1972

This series was ABC's biggest hit up to that time and a star vehicle for Elizabeth Montgomery, who was married to producer William Asher. The story of a mortal marrying a witch, *Bewitched*, like many successful series, can be credited with combining excellent casting, superior writing, and wonderful special effects. Often seen as an allegory for mixed marriages, Samantha and Darrin Stevens powered through repeated attempts by many members of Samantha's family to break them up, because the witches and warlocks felt that a mortal was an inferior companion. Sam kept her gifts secret from nosey neighbors and spying corporate competitors of Darrin's, and *Bewitched* succeeded for eight seasons, surviving many cast changes and overall changes to TV sitcoms in the early 1970s. In 1972, however, Montgomery declined a ninth season, even though ABC wished to continue the series despite its "old-fashioned" premise.

The Stephens Family from *Bewitched*. Dick Sargent, Elizabeth Montgomery, Erin Murphy, David Lawrence, 1971.
ABC

ERIN MURPHY
DIANE MURPHY

(Twins born June 17, 1964)

Character: Tabitha Stevens

Erin, who originally shared the screen with her fraternal twin, Diane, was the daughter of Samantha the witch and Darrin the mortal. She became the sole actor for the character of Tabitha after her first year on the series, in 1966. Erin has told me that she enjoyed her experience on the show, and she has positive thoughts about being a child star. But she did leave show business shortly after the series ended. Erin segued into makeup artistry, modeling, and commercials, but finally gave it all up when she started attending San Diego State. After three marriages and six children (all boys), she decided to return to the biz. She was in the pilot for a new show in 2014 called, ironically, *The Comeback Kids*. She also made the pilot of *Life Interrupted,* where she played the lesbian wife of Alison Arngrim, another former child actor. Alison's character was the ex-wife of the character portrayed by former child star Mason Reese. Erin, other child stars, and I belong to a private Facebook page created by Alison Arngrim that is called the X-Child Actor Secret Society, where we can keep up on the comings and goings and trials and jubilations of our former–child actor sisters and brothers.

The Addams Family

2 Seasons: 65 half-hour episodes

Network: ABC; All episodes black and white

Debut: September 18, 1964 / Finale: April 8, 1966

One theme of the 1964–65 season was fantasy, and *The Addams Family* fit the bill. Like the contemporaneous series *Hazel*, this show was based on a comic strip. Unlike its CBS competitor *The Munsters,* which derived its laughs from a family of monsters in the modern world, the Addamses are a wealthy, supernatural extended family with unusual powers and a flamboyant, if spooky, lifestyle. Stories often centered around the culture clash between the Addamses and the outside world, and despite their general trusting attitude toward strangers with more sinister aims, the family always came out ahead, usually oblivious to any threat. The series was revived as a successful movie franchise in the 1990s.

Cast photo from *The Addams Family*. Lisa Loring (as Wednesday Addams), Jackie Coogan (as Uncle Fester Frump), Carolyn Jones (as Morticia Frump Addams), Marie Blake (as Grandmama Addams), John Astin (as Gomez Addams), Ted Cassidy (as Lurch/Thing), Ken Weatherwax (as Pugsley Addams).

ABC/Photofest

LISA LORING

(Born February 15, 1958)
Character: Wednesday Addams

In the first television rendition of Charles Addams's bizarre cartoons, the character of Wednesday Addams is depicted as an innocent with some strange quirks like an affection for spiders and guillotined headless dolls. It turned out that lovely Lisa had some strange quirks of her own, such as being married and divorced four times and getting involved with some less-than-sterling characters. After some roles in sitcoms and soaps following her childhood appearances, her life became riddled with drugs and the involvement in the pornography industry of her third husband, whom she had met while working as a makeup artist on one of his films. Still intrigued with makeup, she works at a large cosmetics chain, perhaps to mask the turmoil of her life.

KEN WEATHERWAX

(September 29, 1955–December 7, 2014)
Character: Pugsley Addams

Ken Weatherwax was the son of Mac Weatherwax; Mac and his brothers Rudd and Frank were dog trainers who counted Lassie as their most famous trainee. Ken was also the nephew to the famous dancer/actress Ruby Keeler (*42nd Street*). But these connections to show business couldn't save him from being typecast as the character Pugsley, even though the show only lasted two years. The many years in which the show was syndicated and Ken's inability to procure other showbiz jobs or avoid the taunting of school friends frustrated him and led him to enlist in the army at the age of seventeen. After his military service, he went behind the cameras as a grip and set designer. He died of an apparent heart attack at his home in West Hills, California, the victim of his own body and, generally, the wiles of Hollywood.

The Munsters

2 Seasons: 70 half-hour episodes, one unaired pilot

Network: CBS; All episodes black and white; pilot, color

Debut: September 24, 1964 / Finale: May 12, 1966

Creepier and kookier than their ABC rival *The Addams Family*, *The Munsters* was a lighthearted domestic sitcom featuring a suburban family of monsters living in a dark, scary house in the middle of an average American neighborhood in Anytown, USA. The patriarch, Herman, resembled Frankenstein's monster, and his wife, Lily, and her father, Grandpa, were clearly of the vampire set. Herman and Lily spawned a werewolf son. Only poor, hideous Marilyn, a blonde knockout "normal" person by anyone else's tastes, was the outcast of the family. Stories often focused on the family's dismay at how others reacted to their "normal, average American" home. The lighthearted, warm humor of the series was enhanced by perfect casting, and it led to a color theatrical release in 1966 and a reunion TV-movie in 1981.

BUTCH PATRICK

(Born August 2, 1953)

Character: Eddie Munster

The early '60s seemed to spawn strange comedies, and *The Munsters* series was no exception. Butch, born Patrick Allan Lilley, was eleven when, following his appearances in other TV episodic roles, he garnered the role of child werewolf Eddie Munster and costarred with other benign monsters in the macabre household. I have appeared with Butch on many occasions; during one, he told me, "Never let your son wear velvet short pants." When the show ended after two years, he went on to appear as a guest in other episodics until he was chosen as the lead in the Sid and Marty Krofft TV production *Lidsville*, which was also a fantasy series like *The Munsters*. My friend Helen Darras wrote his biography, *Eddie Munster AKA Butch Patrick*. She chronicled his show business career but not his felony drug conviction or his addiction to alcohol, cocaine, and marijuana, which began at approximately sixteen years of age and lasted until he was fifty-seven. At that point, he finally checked himself into rehab after a breakup with his girlfriend. In 2011 Butch was diagnosed with prostate cancer, but he has vowed to fight it. He has been working, making appearances, and living life to the fullest, having finally overcome the child star addiction syndrome.

Please Don't Eat the Daisies

2 Seasons: 58 half-hour episodes

Network: NBC; Color

Debut: September 14, 1965 / Finale: April 22, 1967

Based on Jean Kerr's popular 1957 book and the 1960 hit film of the same name starring Doris Day and David Niven, *Please Don't Eat the Daisies* was a ratings success during its first season, but fell victim to competition by Jackie Gleason with a timeslot change in its second, and ultimately last, season. The premise was fun: An overworked professor and his homebound wife with four children tire of their small city apartment and decide to move to the 'burbs. Stories centered on their adjustment to life as homeowners in their new community.

Set photo from *Please Don't Eat the Daisies*, 1960.
MGM/Photofest

KIM TYLER

(Born April 17, 1954)

Character: Kyle Nash

Kim, the oldest boy of the four in *Please Don't Eat the Daisies*, experienced a short show business career. He appeared as an eighteen-month-old baby on the TV series *Mr. Belvedere* in 1956 before he retired the first time. He made his comeback on an episode of *Ozzie and Harriet* in 1962 before he landed the family sitcom *Please Don't Eat the Daisies*. After the two-year run, Kim retired for good and has since faded into anonymity.

BRIAN NASH

(Born May 20, 1956)
Character: Joel Nash

The next oldest boy in the Nash clan, Brian, shared the same name as his TV family. He had a somewhat longer career than his older brother Kyle did, but not by much. He got his start on *My Three Sons* and garnered small roles on TV episodics before *Please Don't Eat the Daisies* came his way. When the series ended, he continued with guest parts in such shows as *The Wild Wild West* and *Land of the Giants* before his last appearance in 1975 as the character Glenn in the Saturday morning TV series *Isis*. As a Mormon, he went on a mission to South America for two years before returning, settling in Southern California, and taking on a career as a stockbroker. In that profession, as in acting, there are ups and downs, but perhaps in investment one can sometimes reap more stable rewards.

JOE FITHIAN

(Born February 26, 1958)
Character: Tracy Nash

Joe, identical twin to Jeff, began his career at the age of one, working with his brother on commercials. Identical twins are gold-plated in the industry as small children; a company is able to get more production time from these tiny actors by using one after the other for the short time spans permitted by the child labor laws. The regulations served the brothers well when they appeared as a single character in the film *What a Way to Go!* with Shirley MacLaine and Paul Newman. In *Please Don't Eat the Daisies* they were separate characters. But even those separate identities were not enough to encourage them to stay in acting, and the *Please Don't Eat the Daisies* show was their last. They did find entertainment pleasure later in life, however, when they acted as assistant cruise directors guiding vacationers in trivia and other games.

JEFF FITHIAN

(Born February 26, 1958)
Character: Trevor Nash

As Joe's twin and the youngest of five siblings, Jeff found ways to express his own personality even though he joined his brother after *Please Don't Eat the Daisies* as activity directors on cruise lines for twenty years. They now work on dude ranches, but in separate states—one works in Arizona, and one works in Montana.

Lost in Space

3 Seasons: 83 full-hour episodes, and one unaired pilot
Network: CBS; 1965–66, black and white; 1966–68, color
Debut: September 15, 1965 / Finale: March 6, 1968

Later known for producing the great disaster movies of the 1970s, producer Irwin Allen led the adventure genre of the 1960s with a quartet of shows, with *Lost in Space* arguably the most successful one culturally. Facing shortages and crises in the overcrowded future world of 1997, America launches the first family of space explorers to a habitable planet in a nearby solar system. The mission is sabotaged by the evil double agent Dr. Smith, who programs the family's robot to destroy the ship after launch, only to find himself trapped aboard at liftoff. The show began as a thrilling space opera filled with danger and brushes with death as the family made its way on a hostile uncharted planet, but soon Jonathan Harris's take on Dr. Smith turned comical as Batmania brought broad camp comedy into style mid-decade. Despite increasingly outlandish plots and situations, the program remained popular and has lived a long life in syndication.

ANGELA CARTWRIGHT

(Born September 9, 1952)

Character: Penny Robinson

As an entertainment veteran with many credits, including the TV series *Make Room for Daddy* and the film *The Sound of Music*, Angela was primed to don the shiny silvery costume of *Lost in Space*. There was even more to come for this successful child star. Please see her bio under *The Danny Thomas Show*.

BILLY MUMY

(Born February 1, 1954)

Character: Will Robinson

Like Angela, Bill had a nice career going before he was cast as the youngest member of the Robinson family. Beginning at age five in the TV series *Wire Service*, he went on to appear in over thirty-five TV shows, most notably a sterling appearance in *The Twilight Zone* before grabbing the role of Will Robinson. Bill can claim over four hundred television shows and twenty feature films to his credit. His latest is role is in the Marc Zicree's 2015 sci-fi film *Space Command*—he's come full circle from being lost in space! Like Angela, Bill has been able to survive and embrace the entertainment world beyond his childhood. Acting, composing music, playing various instruments, writing (Bill cowrote the TV series *Space Cases*, which ran for two seasons on Nickelodeon in the 1990s, with Peter David), and sustaining a voice-over career has given him satisfaction and financial stability to his wife, Eileen, and two children, Seth and Liliana. Bill has added author to his plethora of credentials with the release of *Lost (And Found) in Space* pictorial edition, which was coauthored by Angela Cartwright. A man of many talents!

Batman

3 Seasons: 120 half-hour episodes, and one unaired *Batgirl* pilot episode

Network: ABC; Color

Debut: January 12, 1966 / Finale: March 14, 1968

Pop culture really didn't enter TV until *Batman* premiered on a cold January night in 1966. In bright primary colors at a time when much of television was still broadcasting in shades of gray, Batman was literally a comic book brought to life while harking back to the days of the movie serials of the 1940s. Airing twice a week during its first two seasons, each *Batman* episode on Wednesday would end with an outlandish cliffhanger of certain death for Batman and Robin by one of the members of their colorful rogues' gallery. Thursday's episode would resolve the threat and capture the criminal, and this formula became an overnight sensation in 1966. It became a status symbol for celebrities to be asked to guest as villains on the program. As the formula tired in 1967, producers attempted to gin up the ratings by adding Yvonne Craig as the curvaceous Batgirl and reducing the number of episodes to one per week in order to speed up the action. Despite the changes, the pop sensation of '66 had tired by '68, and the show quietly bowed out with its final villainess, portrayed by none other than Zsa Zsa Gabor.

BURT WARD

(Born July 6, 1945)

Character: Robin

As a professional ice-skating star from the age of three, Burt had the prowess to take on the athletically-demanding role of the sidekick of the Caped Crusader. So typecast in his part that he found it extremely difficult to get new roles, Burt used his intelligence and energy to write, invest in real estate, and establish charitable organizations such as the Great Dane Rescue. This is one child star who was able to spin his fame around a successful life of continued creativity.

Family Affair

5 Seasons: 138 half-hour episodes

Network: CBS; Color

Debut: September 12, 1966 / Finale: March 4, 1971

Family Affair explores the trials of well-to-do civil engineer and bachelor Bill Davis
(Brian Keith) as he attempted to raise his brother's orphaned children in his luxury
New York City apartment. Davis's traditional English gentleman's gentleman,
Mr. Giles French (Sebastian Cabot), also had adjustments to make as he became
saddled with the responsibility of caring for fifteen-year-old Cissy (Kathy Garver)
and the six-year-old twins, Jody (Johnnie Whitaker) and Buffy (Anissa Jones). The
show was notable for several reasons. It was filmed in color from the beginning
(atypical for the time), and it starred one of the most handsome and sought-after
leading men in motion pictures. Most importantly, it dealt gently but candidly
with the situation that created the family—the fact that a terrible accident had
taken the kids' parents suddenly and with great tragedy. Throughout the run of the
show, the writers never forgot how this family was created and would pay homage

Cast photo from *Family Affair*. Shown: Anissa Jones, Kathy Garver, Johnny Whitaker.

CBS/Photofest

to the special emotions attached to such a loss (compare this with *The Brady Bunch* kids who cheerfully assimilated and never referred to their dead parents—ever!)

During the fifth and final season of the series, Nancy Walker joined the cast as the Davis family's housekeeper and foil for Mr. French. *Family Affair* was created and produced by Don Fedderson, also known for *My Three Sons* and *The Millionaire*.

KATHY GARVER

(Born December 13, 1945)

Character: Catherine Patterson "Cissy" Davis

About the author: Kathy had already appeared in many shows as a child before she gained the coveted role of Cissy. Her debut in the classic film noir *The Night of the Hunter* encouraged her to set her theatrical bar high after working with such stars as Lillian Gish, Robert Mitchum, and Shelley Winters. Her next film also had excellent credentials, as she played the slave girl Rachel in the epic film *The Ten Commandments,* directed by Cecil B. DeMille and starring Charlton Heston, who became her lifelong friend. From there Kathy did most of the episodics of the day and enjoyed a recurring part on the series *This is Alice.* Taking a break to attend high school in San Bernardino, where her father had contracted to design and build homes, she returned to Los Angeles and show business when she began attending UCLA, tucking in appearances in TV episodics along the way.

After she worked for the five years of *Family Affair,* Kathy had many options available to her. She had graduated from UCLA, and she contemplated getting a law degree after being accepted by both Loyola Marymount and UCLA. She was also offered a starring role in a play and a job assisting James Caan in a film he was working on. Ultimately she chose the play. It wasn't long before she bought her first house in Los Angeles near Mulholland Drive. "My parents had dutifully set aside my money in an interest-bearing savings account—even though I was over eighteen when I started the series and they were under no obligation to do so," Kathy recalls. She returned to UCLA to obtain a master's degree in theatre arts and then attended the Royal Academy of Dramatic Art in London. With her stage experience from England, she returned to the states and traveled the country starring in theatrical plays. Kathy then began a successful voice-over career, starring in such animated series as *Spider-Man and His Amazing Friends, Chuck Norris Karate Kommandos,* and *Dixie's Diner* (as Dixie).

She has been married to David Travis since 1981, and they have a son, Reid, who was born in 1991. She continues her work on camera and off, also producing and directing. She wrote her memoir, *Surviving Cissy: My Family Affair of Life in Hollywood,* in 2015 and has two more books contracted. "One of the main reasons I believe I survived the child actors' syndrome," says Kathy, "was because of my parents. Supportive, and not using me as their personal bank, they saved the money I earned even before the Coogan Law required it." She adds, "I also had as normal an upbringing as parents of a child actor could muster. I believe that their handling of my career was another reason I survived the potentially debilitating entertainment whirl."

ANISSA JONES

(March 11, 1958–August 28, 1976)

Character: Buffy Davis

Anissa secured the beginnings of a stalwart acting career by appearing in a commercial for breakfast cereal. On the audition for her first TV role, the producers of *Family Affair* thought her just right for six-year-old Buffy: She was small for her age of eight, adorable, and very intelligent. However, they thought she should remain that little girl throughout the run of the show, even though by the fifth season she was almost fourteen. With her dyed-blond hair still bouncing in childish pigtails, wearing short dresses, Anissa continued to carry around her doll, Mrs. Beasley. By the time the series ended, Anissa had amassed a great deal of money. Her parents, after a contentious divorce in 1965, were battling for custody of her, and Anissa Mary Jones was through with show business. She just wanted to be a "normal" teenager.

She began attending Westchester High near her home at the beach, but unfortunately the teens she befriended there were taking drugs. She began skipping school and got a job at a doughnut shop. I went to her eighteenth birthday party, which was held at her mother Paula's home, and told her worried mom that I was leaving the next day to go to Virginia to star in the musical stage show, *My Fair Lady*, but would get together with Anissa as soon as I returned. The day after her eighteenth birthday, Anissa received her *Family Affair* money from her trust and bonds. Tapping into some of the lucre, she bought a red car for herself and another automobile for her brother. In August of 1976, Anissa went to a weekend party at a friend's house in Oceanside, California. In the early morning, she was found in one of the bedrooms, unconscious. Her teenage friends panicked.

When the medics finally arrived, they found Anissa inert. She had passed away from a lethal cocktail of cocaine, quaaludes, PCP, and Seconal—such a sad ending to the life of a bright, beautiful, and talented girl. Anissa was cremated, and her ashes were spread over the Pacific Ocean near her home in Playa del Rey. It can be dangerous to experience and sometimes very difficult to survive the entertainment business as a child.

JOHNNIE WHITAKER

(Born December 13, 1959)

Character: Jody Patterson Davis

Johnnie's story is similar to Anissa with regard to his struggles with drug and alcohol. His role as Scotty Baldwin in *General Hospital* gave him his initial screen experience, but it was his role in *The Russians Are Coming, the Russians Are Coming* that sealed his fate as Jody in *Family Affair*. Brian Keith starred in this film and, when the handsome man was cast as Uncle Bill, he suggested Johnnie to the producers. They liked him and decided to make Johnnie and Anissa twins even though the boy's role was originally to have been that of a ten-year-old. After *Family Affair*, Johnnie went on to do the TV series *Sigmund and the Sea Monsters* and the movies *Tom Sawyer* and Disney's *Napoleon and Samantha* and *The Snowball Express*. After these roles he went on a Mormon mission; when he returned, he found his bank account almost depleted. After graduating from BYU and experiencing a short-lived marriage and divorce, he was depressed, penniless, and almost homeless. Drug and alcohol abuse followed. His nuclear family did an intervention, and Johnny (as he spells his nickname today) got off drugs. He has been clean and sober ever since. working as a counselor to help others stay off the bad stuff.

Gentle Ben

2 Seasons: 58 half-hour episodes

Network: CBS; Color

Debut: September 10, 1967 / Finale: April 27, 1969

Gentle Ben is one of the last successful series that explored the friendship between a little boy and a wild animal (a la *Lassie* or *The Adventures of Rin Tin Tin*). The premise was simple: Little Mark Wedloe and the rest of his family lived in the Florida Everglades, where they counted on the aid, when necessary, of their great giant of a friend, the black bear Gentle Ben.

CLINT HOWARD

(Born April 20, 1959)

Character: Mark Wedloe

Clint started his acting career by appearing in his brother Ron Howard's series *The Andy Griffith Show*. He then started establishing himself as a steadily working child actor by acting in many episodics and a short-lived series, *The Baileys of Balboa,* before starring in *Gentle Ben*. He has acted in many of Ron's movies both as an on-camera presence, most notably in *Apollo 13,* and as a postproduction voice worker in the ADR (Automated Dialog Replacement) room. I have worked with Clint, I have also cast him for a personal appearance, and I find him to be warm and talented. He has been married to Melanie Howard since 1995, and he spends his spare time playing golf or trying to defeat his opponents in the video game *World of Warcraft*. Clint continues to work in movies and did not seem to find it awkward to go from child to adult acting. I guess it's all in the family.

Maya

1 Season: 18 full-hour episodes

Network: NBC; Color

Debut: September 16, 1967 / Finale: February 10, 1968

Set in the jungles of India, an American boy searches for his missing father, befriending a native in the process. The series was based on the film of the same name from 1966. The title *Maya* is also the name of the boys' elephant and their main mode of transportation.

JAY NORTH

(Born August 3, 1951)

Character: Terry Bowen

Please see Jay's bio under *Dennis the Menace*, page 80.

SAJID KHAN

(Born March 23, 1951)

Character: Raji

While Jay was gaining child stardom in the United States, Sajid was becoming famous for his movie work in India. Adopted by movie producer Meehboob Khan, who also owned Meehboob Studios in Mumbai (Bombay), Sajid gained his first theatrical experience in his father's movies. When *Maya* the movie (filmed in India) was a hit, NBC picked it up to transition into a series. Even though the series only lasted one year, it gave immense US exposure to Sajid, who was already a child star in India. I costarred with Sajid in an episode of *Big Valley*, and I still get fan mail asking what happened to Sajid. Well, after he became a teen idol with his records and starred in some episodics, he moved back to India, did a couple more movies, his last being *Heat and Dust* in 1983, and then quit the business. He eventually established his own jewelry company called Artistic, where he is still working. He was married and divorced once and prefers to go it alone with his elephant companions.

Julia

3 Seasons: 86 half-hour episodes

Network: NBC; Color

Debut: September 17, 1968 / Finale: March 23, 1971

Hard to believe today, but *Julia* was possibly the most groundbreaking program on television in its day. Why? Because it starred an African-American widow (played by Diahann Carroll) working as a nurse while raising her son. Up to that time, there were few, if any, people of color on television at all, much less in starring roles. While the show was tame by today's standards, *Julia* broke the rules and laid the groundwork for Norman Lear and others in the 1970s.

MARC COPAGE

(Born June 21, 1962)

Character: Corey Baker

Winsome child actor Marc Copage snagged the starring part in *Julia* at five years old. "He was so adorable," Ms. Carroll has said of her TV son. Under her tutelage, Marc gained acting chops in the successful show, to go on in the acting world, but ill-advised investments and a lack of roles left him almost penniless seeking success in his profession. Ever affable, Marc picked himself up, took lessons in improvisational music, and now plays in a jazz combo when he isn't "cater waiting" for celebrities. At this writing he is wrapping up his autobiography, *The Adventures of Little Diego* (Diego is Marc's middle name), and lobbying for a spot on *Dancing with the Stars*. There's always hope.

Land of the Giants

2 Seasons: 51 full-hour episodes and one unaired pilot

Network: ABC; Color

Debut: September 22, 1968 / Finale: March 22, 1970

In the distant future of 1983, passengers are able to travel between Los Angeles and London via suborbital flight in less than two hours, that is, unless they find themselves sucked through a warp in space and crashing on the *Land of the Giants*. This Irwin Allen fantasy follows the changeling little people trying to get back to Earth while avoiding the giant-sized population on their new, hostile home.

Cast photo from *Land of the Giants*. Shown from left: front, Gary Conway, Deanna Lund, Kurt Kasznar, Heather Young; back, Don Matheson, Stefan Arngrim, Don Marshall.

ABC/Photofest; Photographer: Gene Trindl

STEFAN ARNGRIM

(Born December 23, 1955)
Character: Barry Lockridge

Accumulating many roles before he landed his starring part in Irwin Allen's highly rated series, Stefan continued his acting career after the show ended. He also began a band with a partner Roland Devoile called Knights of the Living Dead, in which they played from 1986 to 1993. After the Northridge earthquake he and his future wife, Dawn, moved back to Canada, where he was born. Stefan continues not only acting but engaging his musical abilities. These two talents played a large part in Stefan's successful transition from child star to adult actor.

Mayberry R.F.D.

3 Seasons: 78 half-hour episodes

Network: CBS; Color

Debut: September 23, 1968 / Finale: March 29, 1971

Simply stated, this series is a continuation of *The Andy Griffith Show* sans Andy Griffith. The successful formula for the original series was not tested on this homespun sitcom, and the citizens of Mayberry continued about their daily lives until the looming shadow of *All in the Family* and social change led CBS to cancel this series (among many others) while it was still in its prime.

BUDDY FOSTER

(Born July 12, 1957)

Character: Mike Jones

Buddy Foster had a short show business career—well, it *was* difficult being the big brother of ultrafamous Jodie Foster. He did grab a part in the series *Hondo* in addition to his role in *Mayberry R.F.D.*, but he had trouble hanging on and being cast in additional shows after his departure from the spin-off. His last screen appearance was in his sister's movie, *Foxes*, in 1980. Buddy wrote the 1997 biography *Foster Child: An Intimate Biography of Jody Foster*, which detailed his life with his sister and what it was like to be raised by their divorced mother and her lesbian companion. Buddy is now married with two children and at last report was living in Duluth, Minnesota. Jodie has trashed the book as an attempt to get money by using her, but critics have valued the book as a true story that only someone living with the actress/director would know. Having two ex–child stars in a family can be rough going.

Here's Lucy

6 Seasons: 144 half-hour episodes

Network: CBS; Color

Debut: September 23, 1968 / Finale: March 18, 1974

Lucille Ball rebooted *The Lucy Show* in 1968 after selling Desilu to Gulf &
Western and created *Here's Lucy*, a show Lucille Ball Productions would own,
to replace it. In the new series, Gale Gordon was still her boss, but now he was
her brother-in-law, and her real-life children Lucie Arnaz and Desi Arnaz Jr.
portrayed her teenage kids, Kim and Craig. The series followed the standard
Lucy format. It ultimately left the air in 1974, which marked the end of
television's Golden Age.

LUCIE ARNAZ

(Born July 17, 1951)

Character: Kim Carter

Lucie, born into one of the most famous TV families, had to transition not only from child star but to her own personality. She has done an admirable job with charm, savvy, and aplomb. Lucie has also been the caretaker, along with her brother, Desi Jr., of her parent's estate. She has forged her own successful career as producer, writer, entertainer, and mother. Lucie married her second husband, actor/writer/director Laurence Luckinbill, in 1980, and they have three children. Kudos to an ex–child star success. I have played tennis at celebrity tournaments with Lucie; she is charming and a smashing talent with a racket.

DESI ARNAZ JR.

(Born January 19, 1953)

Character: Craig Carter

I had the honor of presenting the *TV Land* Legacy of Laughter award statue to stars Desi Jr. and Lucie onstage, when their mother was proclaimed a queen of comedy. They were gracious and fun-loving, qualities that helped Desi in his passage from actor on his mom's show to drummer in the band Dino, Desi, and Billy, to a respected businessman and producer. He married his second wife, Amy Bargiel, in 1987, after a brief marriage to and divorce from actress Linda Purl. Amy and Desi had a daughter and owned and operated a theatre in Boulder City, Nevada. Amy died in 2015 after a long battle with cancer.

The Doris Day Show

5 Seasons: 128 half-hour episodes

Network: CBS; Color

Debut: September 24, 1968 / Finale: March 12, 1973

Doris Day finally consented to a television series in 1968, and it was greeted with anticipation and enthusiasm. Like *The Lucy Show* that preceded it, *The Doris Day Show* underwent various format changes in its five-year run. The original premise of the show had the widowed Doris raising her two sons on the family ranch in Northern California. By the second season, she was commuting to work in San Francisco every day, and by the third year, she and the boys were moving into the city. In the last two seasons, Doris was a swinging single, with the children nowhere to be found. It is said that Day agreed to do the series to pay off a tax debt, and once that was done, she was done, too.

Todd Starke, Doris Day, and Philip Brown from *The Doris Day Show*, 1968.
CBS/Photofest

PHILIP BROWN

(Born March 26, 1958)

Character: Billy Martin

From small parts in movies, Philip jumped to a big part as one of Doris Day's sons. After his three-year run on the show, he became the king of one-year series from *When the Wind Blows* to *The Colbys*; his series just couldn't catch the fire of at least three years—the minimum for syndication. He remains in the business, however, appearing in commercials; in 2004, he even caught another one-hit wonder in *The Power Rangers Dino Thunder*.

TODD STARKE

(December 19, 1961–May 4, 1983)

Character: Toby Martin

After three years of the five-year run of the series, Toby and his TV brother Billy were released from the show. Todd did an episode of *Adam-12*, but being typecast and disappointed that he had been let go from Day's series had a negative impact on this sensitive boy and colored his feelings toward Hollywood. He did no more work in film or TV and was killed in a tragic motorcycle accident when he was but twenty-one years old.

The Brady Bunch

5 Seasons: 117 half-hour episodes

Network: ABC; Color

Debut: September 26, 1969 / Finale: March 8, 1974

The Brady Bunch is often heralded as the last of the simple domestic sitcoms. Despite the simple premise of the union of a widower with three sons marrying a widow with three daughters, any past grief was forgotten by the time of the first episode's wedding, and the artificial lawn and house with no toilets became a Friday-night staple. After being quietly canceled in 1974, the series has returned many times in many formats. Love them or hate them, the Bradys have earned a place in America's culture and heart.

Brady Bunch stars Barry Williams, Christopher Knight, and Mike Lookinland at the Big Apple Convention in Manhattan, October 1, 2010.
Luigi Novi

BARRY WILLIAMS

(Born September 30, 1953)

Character: Greg Brady

Barry is a success in the ex–child star society. Having an intro into the business early on with parts in TV episodics and movies, he moved on to his success as a TV icon and then to his position as owner and star of the *70s Music Celebration!* stage musical in Branson, Missouri. After two marriages and divorces and a move to the

157

Midwest with his son, he found a way to parlay his past, embrace the present, and plan for the future in the business that he loves.

CHRISTOPHER KNIGHT

(Born November 7, 1957)
Character: Peter Brady

Christopher is another success story from *The Brady Bunch* clan. After the sitcom, Christopher followed his self-proclaimed geekiness and worked for several IT companies in order to garner some financial stability. But once an actor . . . Chris returned to the entertainment world in the 2000s, making several guest appearances and then acquiring a role on the series *The Surreal Life*. There he met Alana Curry, winner of America's Next Top Model, and created his own reality show, *My Fair Brady*, with Alana, whom he married on the series. Now divorced, Chris continues to make guest appearances on shows and work the autograph circuit.

MIKE LOOKINLAND

(Born December 19, 1960)
Character: Bobby Brady

The youngest Brady boy kept his attachment to the original series by appearing in the special *A Very Brady Christmas* and in *The Bradys*, the sequel to the original series.

He moved back to his home state of Utah with his wife, whom he married in 1987, and their two boys, and he now operates a successful decorative concrete business.

MAUREEN McCORMICK

(Born August 5, 1956)
Character: Marcia Brady

It is always heartbreaking when one gets hooked on drugs, but when a beloved, talented child star falls under the influence of cocaine and other illegal substances, it feels especially heinous. The sprightly Maureen who created the perky character of Marcia Brady continued her career after *The Brady Bunch* by appearing in episodic TV shows and ultimately in her own TV shows, including *The Celebrity Fit Club, Gone Country,* and *Outsiders Inn.* She still struggles with depression, but attempts to get past it without the Prozac.

EVE PLUMB

(Born April 29, 1958)
Character: Jan Brady

Eve was an experienced actress, having appeared in numerous commercials and TV episodics, when she was cast as the middle child in the Brady clan, Her love of acting is apparent in the various eclectic roles she has taken on throughout the years, from appearing in Brady reunions, sequels, and films, to her recent work on the New York stage in such plays such as *Miss Abigail's Guide to Dating, Mating and Marriage,* and *Love, Loss and What I Wore.* She successfully made the transition.

SUSAN OLSEN

(Born August 14, 1961)
Character: Cindy Brady

The youngest member of the clan, Susan Olsen, reminds me of my own dear Buffy on *Family Affair*. It is no coincidence. When *Family Affair* was canceled by CBS, producer Don Fedderson pitched the show to ABC. The executives there liked the idea, and the deal was in the works when they were presented with a newer, fresher series. That series, of course, was *The Brady Bunch,* and the youngest daughter could certainly be made to look like the ever-popular Buffy with her iconic pigtails. The hairstyle was established, and the new "Buffy" in the *Brady* show lasted five years. After the end of the series, Susan participated in its reunions and specials and then found herself wanting. Very creative, she turned to art and graphic design while hosting a radio show in Los Angeles. She now devotes much of her time helping to rescue animals as a board member for the nonprofit group Precious Paws.

THE 1970s

The Partridge Family

4 Seasons: 96 half-hour episodes

Network: ABC; Color

Debut: September 25, 1970 / Finale: March 23, 1974

The Partridge Family was originally conceived as a series for real-life family band The Cowsills, who were very popular in the late 1960s. When a deal couldn't be reached with them, the fictitious Partridge Family was created, led by real-life stepmother and son singers Shirley Jones and David Cassidy and complemented by a talented young cast to complete the family. The series begins several months after the family's father has died, and finances are a problem. The kids decide they can help out by forming a band to supplement their mom's income, and they become an overnight sensation. Stories are of the usual domestic comedy sort; an original song is thrown in before the end of every episode and typically relates to the episode's plot.

A set shot from *The Partridge Family*. Shown from left: Susan Dey, Brian Forster, Shirley Jones, Danny Bonaduce.
ABC/Photofest

DAVID CASSIDY

(Born April 12, 1950)

Character: Keith Partridge

It's tough being a pop idol! It's also hard being the son of Jack Cassidy and having your stepmother play your real mother on a family sitcom. David Cassidy had these issues to deal with. However, upon leaving a series, it was a good thing to have your father's manager take over your career, renegotiate contracts, and secure on-camera jobs. David sold millions of albums, invested in Thoroughbred horses, and bought real estate. But then . . . he was arrested three times for DUI, and he declared bankruptcy in 2015. David has been married and divorced three times and has two children. Now he is out of rehab and continuing on a worldwide performing tour—maybe some of those tickets can buy him back onto the road of success.

DANNY BONADUCE

(Born August 13, 1959)

Character: Danny Partridge

As the middle child in the Partridge family, Danny made his presence known by blasting his personality as a smart-alecky kid and his loud music as the bass player into the show. When the series ended, Danny went through some rough times; he found himself homeless, living in his car, and abusing drugs and alcohol. He was arrested for attempting to buy cocaine from an undercover officer and then for robbing and beating a transvestite prostitute. In the '80s and '90s he found work as a radio disc jockey, in reality shows, and occasionally as an actor in episodic TV. After two stormy marriages, he is now clean and sober and married to Amy Railsback, who acts as his manager and oversees their company, Gravel Tones productions. It has indeed been a stony road for him.

SUSAN DEY

(Born December 10, 1952)

Character: Laurie Partridge

Susan's first main acting role as the beautiful Laurie Partridge grew out of her experience as a teen model. Having reached the magic age of eighteen, Susan was able to work the long hours required for a top sitcom. The show was difficult on her, and she became anorexic, supposedly eating only carrots on occasion. After the show ended, I once visited her at her canyon house on the outskirts of Beverly Hills; she had just given birth to her beautiful baby girl, Sara. Susan was quite nice, but I sensed a sadness in her. Three years later she divorced her much-older husband, famed William Morris agent Leonard Hirshan. Susan captured another successful series, *LA Law*, and was lauded for her role; she won the Golden Globe award for her performance in 1987. A year later she married the creator and producer of that award show, Bernard Sofronski. She has taken on some parts since the demise of *LA Law* and appeared in two of her husband's films. When you are married to a very successful producer of film, TV, and award shows, it is much easier to make the transition from child star.

SUZANNE CROUGH

(March 6, 1963–April 27, 2015)
Character: Tracy Partridge

Redheaded, vivacious Suzanne was a natural for commercials, which she continued to do even while *The Partridge Family* was shooting. Suzanne was one of the few Partridge children who actually played her instrument, thrumming her tambourine while pounding on the keyboards. When the series wrapped, she continued acting in parts on TV and attended cast-reunion shows. Susan Dey had repeatedly turned down those reminders of the past. By 1980 Suzanne was through with showbiz and opened a bookstore in Temecula, California, which she owned and operated until 1993. Moving to Bullhead, Arizona, with her lawyer-husband, Bill, and two daughters, Samantha and Alexandra, she died unexpectedly in April 2015 at the age of fifty-two; it seemed that she had put her head on a table and just fallen asleep. But a medical incident had occurred, perhaps from a rare heart condition, perhaps from something else; some speculated that it was brought on by the extreme stress of financial obligations that had the IRS repeatedly banging on her door.

JEREMY GELBWAKS

(Born May 22, 1961)
Character: Chris Partridge I

Jeremy was the first embodiment of the character of Chris Partridge. After only one season of shooting the series, Jeremy's "real" family reigned supreme: His father was transferred to Reston, Virginia, and the tribe followed. Although Jeremy has iterated some "what ifs" ("I coulda been a star"), he found happiness and success not on the big screen but on that small one we use so often—the computer. After studying chemistry at UC–Berkeley in 1983, he became a computer analyst and went to work for a major technical services company. Sometimes it's nice to have a steady job.

BRIAN FORSTER

(Born April 14, 1960)
Character: Chris Partridge II

Brian seemed to be the apt replacement for Jeremy. Brian had to his credit over twenty commercials, TV roles, and a litany of creative successful relatives in his background, including his actor father Peter Forster, uncle Alan Napier (Alfred the butler in *Batman*), and author/actor Charles Dickens as his great-great-great-grandfather. With a family cast list like that in his life, he definitely had an advantage over other acting candidates. Plus he was cute as a button. He had one audition for the role with the producers and director, and he was in. Brian seamlessly took on the role as drummer in the family band, and another TV child actor icon was born. However, the job wasn't as much fun as he had hoped. I believe he had a more enjoyable time when he appeared in an episode of *Family Affair* and got to play with the elephant we had brought to the set for one taping. Brian left showbiz and began a faster career track as a race car driver. I did an interview with him at his home in Sebastopol in 2009. He told me his mother wasn't thrilled that he left show business for race car driving, even though she had always directed him away from the entertainment world with the dictum that he was only acting to save money for college. Brian embraced the tamer life of teaching school for a while. He is now a husband and a stepfather. His newest endeavor is working in the heady tasting room of a vineyard—he lives in the intoxicating wine country of Northern California. Brian still treads the boards of the local stage occasionally and plays a guitar, but his heart is in the relative anonymity of smelling the wafting waves of fermenting grapes in NorCal.

The Mary Tyler Moore Show

7 Seasons: 168 half-hour episodes

Network: CBS; Color

Debut: September 19, 1970 / Finale: March 19, 1977

The first run-through of filming the pilot to *Mary Tyler Moore* in front of a live audience was a bomb. There were reportedly few laughs, and the characters were found to be abrasive and disagreeable. The premise of the show centered on a thirty-year-old single woman moving to a new city to start a new life after the breakup of a long-term relationship, and the series split its time between Mary's friendships at home with neighbors Rhoda and Phyllis and her interactions at work in an all-male newsroom helmed by a gruff, hard-drinking producer. Mary and husband/producer Grant Tinker reworked the script, fearing they had really misfired on the concept. What changed? Little Lisa Gerritsen, cast as the young daughter of Mary's neighbor and friend Phyllis, was added to the scene that introduced Rhoda, a harsh New Yorker angry at Phyllis for renting the apartment to Mary instead of her. At the end of the scene, as Phyllis and her daughter exit,

Lisa Gerritsen as Bess Lindstrom from *The Mary Tyler Moore Show*, 1975.
CBS

Lisa says to Mary, "I really like Rhoda!" And that made the audience like Rhoda. And suddenly it all came together.

The Mary Tyler Moore Show was a trailblazing sitcom with a hint of what was to come in just a few months with the premiere of *All in the Family* on the same network. The concept of the single girl had not gone further than Marlo Thomas's cute *That Girl*, and while *Mary* began on the tame side, as the decade progressed, so did its grasp on the issues of the day and the hearts of viewers. Ultimately the show spawned three direct spin-offs and launched successful careers for virtually the entire cast.

LISA GERRITSEN

(Born December 27, 1957)

Character: Bess Lindstrom

I first met Lisa on the set of *Family Affair* where she was playing Anissa Jones's (Buffy) friend. I was immediately taken with her verve and spirit. Lisa had appeared in episodics before and after *Family Affair,* but her big break came in securing a role in the short-lived but critically acclaimed TV series *My World and Welcome to It* starring Emmy-winning actor William Windom, another personal favorite of mine. The next year she landed on *The Mary Tyler Moore Show* sporadically and then regularly on the spin-off show *Phyllis* from 1975 to 1977. Lisa was an intelligent and talented child and went on to do such movies as *Airport* and *The War Between Men and Women* alongside such luminaries as Jack Lemmon and Barbara Harris, but her last appearance was on the spiritual show *Insight*. She voluntarily left the business at twenty-one, went to college, and now leads a quiet life in Northern California with her husband, whom she married in 2000, and a son. When last heard from, she was an independent location consultant and facilities project manager, a job she attained after having worked for a couple of software companies. She always was a smart person. Sometimes, a long career in show business isn't for everyone, even if a smooth transition from child star to adult actor is achieved.

All in the Family /
Archie Bunker's Place

13 Seasons: 210 episodes for *All in the Family* and 97 episodes for *Archie Bunker's Place*

Network: CBS; Color

Debut: January 12, 1971 / Finale: April 4, 1983

I Love Lucy can be credited with creating the successful domestic sitcom format that dominated the 1950s and 1960s, and *All in the Family* is the show that broke the mold and reinvented the sitcom and episodic content. Prior to producer Norman Lear's program's debut, which took four years to get on the air, the world of TV was largely in a bubble that ignored the social, cultural, and political upheaval of the late 1960s and early 1970s. Even the devastating Vietnam War was rarely mentioned, even on military sitcoms such as *Gomer Pyle, U.S.M.C.*

On January 12, 1971, CBS aired the first episode at 10:30 p.m. and issued a warning prior to its debut to warn viewers of objectionable content. Expecting a widely negative response, CBS reportedly only received five complaints that night about the iconic show. By summer, the program was a hit, and since then sitcoms have dealt with serious issues such as abortion, menopause, and adultery.

By fall, CBS had canceled "every program with a tree in it" and begun retooling its programming in the image of Norman Lear. *All in the Family* itself led to seven spin-offs; as such its influence reached into the 1990s.

DANIELLE BRISEBOIS

(Born June 28, 1969)

Character: Stephanie Mills

Danielle joined *All in the Family* in 1978 and then moved over to *Archie Bunker's Place* from 1979 to 1983. The pretty brunette was heralded as an excellent actress; she won two Young Artist's awards and a Golden Globe for her portrayal of the young Stephanie in *Archie's Bunker Place*. Music held more sway than acting in Danielle's playbook, however, and she became a lauded songwriter and musician. In 2015 she was nominated for an Academy Award for "Lost Stars," from the movie *Begin Again*, which she cowrote and produced with her writing team. Her memorable melodies continue in her marriage and with her twin girls, who were born in 2013.

The Waltons

9 Seasons: 210 episodes

Network: CBS; Color

Debut: September 14, 1972 / Finale: June 4, 1981

President George H. W. Bush once remarked that American families should aspire to be like the Waltons, not the Simpsons. Indeed, *The Waltons* was initially centered on the struggles of a large family living in the mountains of Virginia in the depths of the Great Depression. Over the years, as the family grew and times changed, the focus moved to American life during World War II. An excellent cast and exceptional writing keep this show fresh forty years later, and six reunion movies after the series ended aired into the late 1990s.

A day of thanks on Walton's Mountain. *The Waltons*, 1982
NBC/Photofest

RICHARD THOMAS

(Born June 13, 1951)

Character: John-Boy Walton

Award-winning former child actor Richard has enjoyed an excellent career in the entertainment field. He made his acting debut onstage playing the son of Franklin Delano Roosevelt in *Sunrise at Campobello*, his initiation into historic roles. As John-Boy Walton, a role he secured in the '70s as actor and narrator for Earl Hamner's true-life story, Richard put his experience to good use. He was nominated and won the Emmy award in 1973 for Outstanding Continued Performance by an Actor in a Leading Role (Drama Series–Continuing). After the series he continued to play interesting roles in TV-movies and onstage, including roles on Broadway in Lanford Wilson's *Fifth of July* and David Mamet's *Race*. He galloped back to the small screen to appear in the role of Frank Gaad on the FX series *The Americans*, true to his *Waltons* roots. He is married to Georgina Bischoff, and the couple has one son. Thomas's older son and triplet daughters are from his first marriage to Alma Gonzales.

JON WALMSLEY

(Born February 6, 1956)
Character: Jason Walton

Although born in Lancaster, England, Jon quickly became Americanized and played one of the country boys in the rural series for nine years. He even married his "reel" wife in the show, Lisa Harrison, who played Toni Hazelton. After the show, he turned his talents to the world of music and became proficient in a multitude of instruments (he could have been a member of the musical Partridge family but he really did know how to play), including piano, guitar, cello, and percussion. Rediscovering his original roots, he now plays in the '60s-genre British rock band, UK Beat. He found his own marital beat with his second wife, Marion Walmsley, whom he met on tour in Bavaria. He has a daughter from his first marriage.

ERIC SCOTT

(Born October 20, 1958)
Character: Ben Walton

Like his costar Kami Cotler, Eric limited his acting career primarily to *Waltons* appearances. From the 1971 *The Homecoming: A Christmas Story* to the 1997 *A Walton's Easter,* he essayed the role of Ben with folksy appeal. He is married to his third wife, Cindy Wolfen, and they have two children. Eric also has a daughter, Ashley, by his second wife, Theresa Fargo, who unfortunately contracted leukemia during her pregnancy and died. Opting for the business world, Eric founded a successful delivery service called Chase Messengers. He may be based in Los Angeles close to the entertainment capital, but the Hollywood Hills aren't for everyone.

DAVID HARPER

(Born October 4, 1961)
Character: Jim Bob Walton

Now known officially as David W. Harper, the actor left show business after a couple of post-*Waltons* attempts in television. After a series of odd jobs, including working for his "reel" brother Eric Scott's messenger service, David returned to school to study business. He participated in the TV reunion specials and attends memorabilia fairs and meet-and-greets, but that is the limit of his entertainment involvement. As a religious person, he has followed his spirit and heart away from Walton's Mountain, and he continues to scale different heights.

JUDY NORTON

(Born January 29, 1958)

Character: Mary Ellen Walton

One of our successful actors who made the transition from child star is well-rounded Judy Norton, who got her theatrical feet wet onstage at the age of seven. Her singing and acting training held her in good stead as she worked in TV episodics and other film fare until she landed the role of Mary Ellen in the long-running *Waltons* series. When the show ended, she extended her athletic prowess by skydiving, playing basketball, and skiing. With her second husband, she ran dinner theatres in Canada and acted in the shows. Judy wrote and starred in the indie film *Finding*. She presently is writing, directing, and acting in the Canadian TV series *Bluff*. Yes, Judy definitely has been able to utilize her talents to prolong her career in many aspects of the entertainment business. Kudos, singer/writer/director/actor Judy!

MARY ELIZABETH McDONOUGH

(Born May 4, 1961)

Character: Erin Walton

Mary, like Judy, got a big boost to her career when she appeared on the pilot special *The Homecoming: Christmas* and segued into the role of Erin for the nine years of *The Waltons*. But after the show she fell victim to the pressures of Hollywood and its demands. Mary has said that during the era of *Dallas* and big hair, she felt she had to fit into the Hollywood mold. She lost weight on questionable diets and succumbed to the idealized body image of the time by getting breast implants. She claims the implants leaked silicone and caused her to contract lupus, an autoimmune disease. Writing as Mary McDonough, she chronicled her fate in her 2012 memoir, *Lessons from the Mountain: What I Learned from Erin Walton*; she stated that many of her woes came from a false notion that she needed to change her image to gain more work and acceptance. She claimed that she had low esteem on the series and found it difficult to adjust when the show ended. As a divorcée and newly single mom, she rebuilt her life as a motivational speaker. She is now remarried and in 2015 released her second book, *One Year*, a fictional tale about the lives of three generations of Irish American women living in Virginia.

KAMI COTLER

(Born June 17, 1965)
Character: Elizabeth Walton

Kami's child-star career was primarily centered on her *Waltons* family. Besides the pilot and nine years on the show, she also appeared as the youngest Walton on *The Waltons: A Decade of the Waltons, A Day for Thanks on Walton's Mountain, Mother's Day*, and *A Wedding on Walton's Mountain* in the 1980s. She returned as her character to appear in *A Walton Thanksgiving, Reunion, Wedding,* and *Easter* in the 1990s and so finished her role in Earl Hamner Jr.'s country film panorama. Eschewing the theatrical world for academia, Kami graduated from UC–Berkeley and after many teaching stints created the Environmental Charter Middle School in Gardena, California. She is happily married with two children.

KEITH COOGAN

(Born January 13, 1970)
Character: Jeffrey Burton

The grandson of famed Jackie Coogan, Keith was named for his father; his
mother is actress Leslie Diane Coogan. Keith was billed as Keith Mitchell, but
when Jackie Coogan died, Keith reverted to his family name, he has stated, out
of respect to the elder star. Apparently inheriting some of his relative's excellent
acting talent, he was lassoed into the *Waltons* franchise when he was nine years
old, in the second to last season of the show. He stayed until the final episode in
1981. Playing the role of mischievous Jeffrey Burton, he enjoyed his stint on the
series and went on to appear in several more episodics and family films, including
Adventures in Babysitting. He is still working in TV and films and writes several
blogs. Threads of talent are hard to break.

MARTHA NIX

(Born September 26, 1967)
Character: Serena Burton

Martha, who played the sister of Jeffrey Burton, also entered the *Waltons* realm
in the 1979 season, after beginning her career on *Days of Our Lives* at the age
of seven. Her early entry into the entertainment world proved to be quite
unsettling. In 2008 she wrote *My Secret Life: A Truthful Look at a Child Actor's
Victory over Sexual Abuse,* in which she reveals that she was molested during her

time on *The Waltons* and afterward by a Sunday-school teacher. Keeping the secret and disassociating herself from these traumatic occurrences naturally affected her film and personal lives in a negative way. Now recovered and helping others to do the same, as well as educating the public on the horrors of these unthinkable crimes, she began the nonprofit A Quarter Blue. Its mission is protecting children, restoring lives, and helping families. Martha Nix Wade continues her work, which has helped and continues to help many who have been caught in the tortuous web of sexual abuse.

Happy Days

11 Seasons: 255 episodes

Network: ABC; Color

Debut: January 15, 1974 / Finale: September 24, 1984

Three years after the launch of controversial programming such as *All in the Family*, *Maude,* and other shows produced or influenced by Norman Lear, American viewers were ready for a change of pace. While those other "message" shows continued to dominate the ratings and viewers, *Happy Days* offered a period sitcom set in 1950s suburban Milwaukee and followed the lives of three high school boys as they made their way into the world. Intentionally mocking the stereotypical nuclear family ideal of the '50s, beneath the surface the humor exposed how shallow and un-ideal that time period truly was. The show, a spin-off of a sketch piece from a 1971 episode of *Love, American Style*, was only moderately successful at first. However, when the character of slick, leather-clad local hood "The Fonz" was expanded, the show zoomed to number one and spawned a half-dozen spin-offs, including superhits *Laverne & Shirley* and *Mork & Mindy*.

The cast of *Happy Days*. From left: Ron Howard, Anson Williams, Henry Winkler, Don Most.
ABC/Photofest; Photographer: David Sutton

RON HOWARD

(Born March 1, 1954)

Character: Richie Cunningham

This is one of the big ex–child star success stories. Not succumbing to drugs, typecasting, or cynicism, Ron was able to forge a successful adult career as writer, director, producer, and loving father and husband. His stable family has been accredited to his success as well as his own motivation and drive to create the best. Ron came from a showbiz family; his father, Rance, attended drama school at Oklahoma University and was featured in plays, films, and as Howard

Broomhauer in the TV series *Gentle Ben,* which also starred his younger son, Clint Howard. Acting genes certainly were passed on to Ron. Besides his initial work on *The Andy Griffith Show*, Ron enjoyed fame in *Happy Days* and then as a respected director and producer in film and television. Some of his award-winning movies include *Apollo 13*, *Backdraft, EDtv* and *Parenthood*, for which I, Kathy, your humble author worked under Ron's direction in postproduction as part of the loop group. His 2002 film *A Beautiful Mind* won him the Oscar for directing and producing.

For additional information, please see Ron Howard's bio under *The Andy Griffith Show*. Ron produced the TV series *Arrested Development*; he also narrated and appeared on the show at times. There's a bit of irony here: This talented adult is a great example of how early childhood stardom doesn't necessarily lead to arrested development in real life.

ERIN MORAN

(Born October 18, 1960)

Character: Joanie Cunningham

Erin Moran, on the other hand, is an example of arrested development. The cute Erin had many shows under her talented belt before she was chosen to play Richie's younger sister. After her role as Jenny Jones on the *Daktari* series in 1968, she guest-starred on *The Courtship of Eddie's Father, My Three Sons,* and even *Family Affair,* as Anissa's friend. The spin-off attempt of *Joanie Loves Chachi* in 1982 did well but not well enough, and she was back on *Happy Days* until its end. After *Happy Days* literally jumped the shark, she guest-starred on some TV shows. But more recently, when I've seen her at some autograph shows, Erin has seemed very hyper and "overmedicated." She hit the news grid with her homelessness, but has since been under the grid, even though fellow actors have tried to help. Now we can only pray.

HENRY WINKLER

(Born October 30, 1945)
Character: Arthur "The Fonz" Fonzarelli

Henry is included in this book because he began his career in kindergarten as "'toothpaste' in a hygiene skit." He is also involved in many children's charities; he was honored with an OBE (Order of the British Empire) award given by Queen Elizabeth II for his work with learning-challenged British children through his My Way! Campaign. Henry has also written a series of children's books about a fourth-grader with dyslexia (from which Henry at thirty-one discovered that he himself suffered) titled *Hank Zipzer: The World's Greatest Underachiever.*

A graduate of Emerson College and later Yale Drama School, Henry was able to override his dyslexia and conquer academic challenges. He also conquered the financial world of showbiz by accepting lower pay for his work in *Happy Days* for a piece of the series. Very smart, Mr. Winkler! When *Happy Days* started to fall in the ratings, Fonzie was shown in an episode where he water-skis over a shark; based on that scene, "jumping the shark" came to mean that a series was on its last breath. But Henry's breathing was strong after the cancellation of the show, and he went on to become famous for directing and producing TV and film. He has resumed an on-camera presence, acting in such shows as *Arrested Development, Royal Pains,* and

Parks and Recreation, and is a regular on *Childrens Hospital*. Henry and his wife, Stacey, have been married since 1978, and they have two children of their own plus Stacey's son by a previous marriage. Kudos to a successful "ex–child star"!

ANSON WILLIAMS

(Born September 25, 1949)
Character: Potsie Weber

Potsie was already past twenty-one when he began his TV role as a teenager. But since it is said that the brain isn't finished growing until a person reaches the age of twenty-five, Anson gets full fare here as an ex–child star. Also, many times adults are chosen to play teenagers because of the child labor laws concerning actors under eighteen. Anson's first foray into showbiz actually was at the age of twenty-one, on an episode of *Owen Marshall, Counselor at Law*. He segued to other episodics before he was cast in his iconic role. Like Henry Winkler he found more satisfaction behind the camera and became a successful director on such TV shows as *Sabrina the Teenage Witch, Star Trek: Deep Space 9,* and *Beverly Hills 90210*. For five years, he was the primary director for *The Secret Life of the American Teenager*. The ability to go in a different direction began when he was on the series and he partnered with fellow actor Al Molinaro to open a string of eateries called Al's Diner. He continues this entrepreneurial spirit with his co-ownership of StarMaker Cosmetics and Physicians Prefer, the latter a company that specializes in "drug-free solutions to debilitating problems," according to his LinkedIn profile. He is also the author of a 2014 memoir: *Singing to a Bulldog: From "Happy Days" to Hollywood Director, and the Unlikely Mentor Who*

Got Me There. Anson has been married since 1988; he and his wife, Jackie, have four children. Our talented "teenager" is a successful Renaissance man.

DON MOST

(Born August 8, 1953)
Character: Ralph Malph

Dropping out of high school and moving from Flatbush to Los Angeles was Don Most's path to join the group on *Happy Days*, where he was billed as either Donny Most or Donald Most. He originally interviewed for the part of Richie Cunningham, but he lost out to Ron Howard and accepted the role of Ralph Malph. When the show was canceled, he continued on as guest star in TV episodics and regained some of the education he lost by going to Lehigh University in Bethlehem, Pennsylvania. Moving back to Los Angeles, he garnered additional roles in TV and movies and voiced such animated series as *Dungeons and Dragons* and *Teen Wolf*. He and his wife, Morgan, have been married since 1982 and have two daughters. In 2011 Don was part of a lawsuit with Anson Williams, Marion Ross, and Erin Moran against CBS. The suit complained that the actors had not been given what were they were owed for merchandising. They settled out of court, reportedly for $65,000 each. Don added directing and producing to his theatrical file and then singing to his acting career. That addition helped him maintain a presence in the showbiz world. He now tours with a cabaret act, *Donny Most Sings and Swings*, which includes songs originally sung by Frank Sinatra, Bobby Darin, and Dean Martin, with reminiscences about his life on *Happy Days*. It's hard to let a good thing go.

SCOTT BAIO

(Born September 22, 1960)

Character: Chachi Arcola

Scott has been a mainstay actor ever since he started working in commercials as a child. At sixteen he was cast in the children's gangster movie *Bugsy Malone* along with Jodie Foster. The publicity from that film helped him land an interview with Gary Marshall to play the Fonz's cousin and join the *Happy Days* gang. With that new role, Scott's popularity soared. Moving from New York to Los Angeles, he could then skip from movie to movie (*Skatetown* and *Zapped*), and TV series (*Blansky's Beauties* and *Who's Watching the Kids?*), while still working on *Happy Days*. He even slipped in his own series, *Joanie Loves Chachi,* which lasted just seventeen episodes. After *Happy Days* was canceled Scott immediately retained another successful series, *Charles in Charge*. He had already been rated as a teen idol, and the new role certainly helped maintain his image. When that show was canceled, he went on to star in movies and appear on TV shows as well as reality series such as *Scott Baio Is 45 . . . and Single*. He is now married to Renee after his escapades with a series of beauties and they have a daughter, Bailey DeLuca. Scott continues to star and work in Hollywood; his latest series, *See Dad Run*, is on Nick at Nite and is produced by Scott. He exemplifies that refraining from drugs and alcohol can help tame the Hollywood beast and enable a child star, teen idol, and adult actor to fulfill his greatest potential.

Land of the Lost

3 Seasons: 43 episodes

Network: NBC; Color

Debut: September 7, 1974 / Finale: December 4, 1976

Sid and Marty Krofft dominated Saturday morning television for much of the 1970s, but of all their hits, the most enduring—and complex—series was *Land of the Lost*. While on a rafting expedition, Rick Marshall and his teenage son (played by adult actor Wesley Eure) and daughter (played by Kathy Coleman) find themselves stranded in a lost world inhabited by both dinosaurs and futuristic creatures. Tales of time travel, alternate realities, and human survival made this a hit among children and adults alike.

KATHY COLEMAN

(Born February 18, 1962)
Character: Holly Marshall

Kathy did commercials and sang with the Mike Curb Congregation from 1972 to 1973 before she was chosen at age fourteen to play the part of Holly in this Saturday-morning children's program. She has stated that she had a good time filming the TV series, but when it was over, she found it difficult to find work. Adult Kathleen has surmised that it was because she was sixteen and of a normal height; producers and casting agents would hire eighteen-year-olds who looked younger and could work longer to play the roles she would have gotten. Instead she married at eighteen into the Bell family (the settlers of Bel Air), had two sons, and moved to the Bells' dairy ranch in Fallon, Nevada. After divorce, struggles with drugs and alcohol, an abusive relationship, and a partnership of twelve years, she is living alone in a trailer but eager to get back into acting and proud that she is now independent. Her memoir, *Lost Girl: The Truth and Nothing but the Truth So Help Me Kathleen*, was published in 2015.

Little House on the Prairie / Little House: A New Beginning

9 Seasons: 204 episodes

Network: NBC; Color

Debut: September 11, 1974 / Finale: March 21, 1983

The popular series of *Little House* books by Laura Ingalls Wilder (based on her real-life family) has been a staple of adolescent reading since the 1930s, so it was a natural candidate to inspire a television series. The *Little House* series followed the lives of the homesteader Ingalls family on the prairies of the Midwest in the 1870s and 1880s. Not truly a Western and not exactly in the mold of *The Waltons*, *Little House* depicted the reality of the hardships faced by those brave enough to settle the West in the nineteenth century. Infant mortality was high, childhood fevers could lead to adolescent blindness, and a financial panic could quickly turn a village into a ghost town.

A cast shot from *Little House on the Prairie*. Shown clockwise from left: Melissa Sue Anderson, Karen Grassles, Michael Landon, Melissa Gilbert, Lindsay/Sidney Greenbush; below: Jack.

NBC/Photofest

MELISSA GILBERT

(Born May 8, 1964)

Character: Laura Ingalls Wilder

As a fixture on TV series and TV-movies, Melissa worked steadily after she began her career on Santa's lap as the little girl in *The Dean Martin Show*. After her starring role on the series, Melissa continued her acting career, supplanting it with directorial and producing duties. For a while she tried to help actors when she served as president of the Screen Actors Guild (2001–2005). Finding that politics was not really to her liking, she resumed her theatrical career while raising her two stepsons, Lee and Sam Boxleitner, and sons, Dakota and Michael. Melissa and her third husband, Timothy Busfield, live in Michigan, where she writes and cares for her family. Her books include *My Prairie Cookbook* and the children's book *Daisy and Josephine*. In her 2009 book, *Prairie Tale: A Memoir,* she reveals her trials with alcohol and drugs, which underlines the fact that even successful child stars who have crossed over to successful adult careers are still faced with such typical Hollywood stresses as addiction, politics, multiple relationships, and tax problems.

MELISSA SUE ANDERSON

(Born September 26, 1962)

Character: Mary Ingalls Kendall

This award-winning actress enjoyed her stint on *Little House* and wrote the book *The Way I See It: A Look Back at My Life on Little House* in 2010, in which she regales her readers with anecdotes about her fellow cast members and crew. It seems Michael Landon was especially taken with the young actress, as he requested her services in his autobiographical film *The Loneliest Runner* in 1976. Melissa continued her career when she left the show after seven years (appearing twice in the eighth season). Appearances in film and TV followed until she married Michael Sloan, creator of the TV show *The Equalizer*, and moved to Canada, where she is a dual citizen. The couple has two children, Piper and Griffin. Now semiretired, Melissa enjoys her family and memories of a successful show and equally successful transitioning.

MATTHEW LABYORTEAUX

(Born December 8, 1966)

Character: Albert (Quinn) Ingalls

Matthew acted in some episodic TV shows before he garnered the role of Albert, the adopted brother of Laura Ingalls Wilder, in the series. Perhaps there was a bond between his character and Matthew because he had also been adopted in real life. Overcoming the difficulties of autism and born with a hole in his heart, Matt has been quite successful in his career; he has followed his passion for video games, having won several contests, and provided voices for games, TV, and film. He and his younger brother Patrick Labyorteaux, who also appeared in *Little House*, founded the Youth Rescue Fund, which helps runaway children and provides shelter for them. Matt evidently found a way to shelter himself from the potentially dangerous throes of Hollywood and child acting.

LINDSAY GREENBUSH
SIDNEY GREENBUSH

(Twins born on May 25, 1970)

Character: Carrie Ingalls

Identical twins Lindsay and Sidney had done a Doublemint commercial and appeared in the TV-movie *Sunshine* before the producer of that film recommended them to Michael Landon, who in turn deemed them just right to star as the youngest member of the Ingalls clan. After almost nine years on the series, the girls struggled to find work in Hollywood and tired of the acting realm altogether; they decided to quit show business and pursue other venues. Lindsay has a daughter, Katelynn, born in 1995, and she married her husband, Frank Dornan, in 2001. She still acts occasionally but is primarily a horse trainer in Simi Valley, California, and works for the Kid Gloves Boxing Foundation. Her older sister (by three minutes) Sidney was married for nine years to William "Rocky" Foster before he took his own life. She now competes in women's professional rodeo and trains and consigns horses at her ranch in Little Rock, California. Still together in TV history, the twins have each gone on from their prairie beginnings to find interesting equine careers.

ALISON ARNGRIM

(Born January 18, 1962)

Character: Nellie Oleson

Alison Arngrim has stated that playing the role of mean and nasty Nellie Oleson was great therapy for her. In her 2010 memoir, *Confessions of a Prairie Bitch: How*

I Survived Nellie Oleson and Learned to Love Being Hated, she chronicled childhood abuse by her brother and how she was able to fight through it by acting out in her dramatic roles. Asked if she ever regretted being on the show, she said, "One half of one percent of people are ever so lucky to be on a successful series. I'm happy to have been one of those one and a half percents!" Alison continues her successful career by acting in TV and film and touring her one-woman show internationally. Overcoming emotional hardships, Alison succeeded in finding happiness in her work and with her marriage to musician Robert Schoonover, whom she met at an event for the Southern California AIDS Hotline. Alison devotes much of her time to worthwhile charities.

JONATHAN GILBERT

(Born July 10, 1968)
Character: Willie Oleson

Jonathan Gilbert, younger adopted brother of Melissa, appeared throughout the run of *Little House*. It was to be his only theatrical run (besides an appearance in 1979 on the TV-movie *The Miracle Worker*). When the series was canceled, he fled to the East Coast and attended Hamilton College, where he earned a BA in business. He then attained his master's degree at Baruch College and became a stock broker. The financial side of life was more appealing to him than the bright lights of Hollywood or the dim lights of candles on the prairie. He now lets his own inner light shine.

RADAMES PERA

(Born September 14, 1960)

Character: John Sanderson Edwards

Radames had a nice acting résumé by the time he was cast as the fiancé of Mary Ingalls. From the beginning of his career, in the role of the dying son of Anthony Quinn in *A Dream of Kings*, he gained a reputation for being able to play dramatic roles. He was also cast as Young Grasshopper in the TV show *Kung Fu*. The reputation did not work to his favor as he tried to make the transition to adult actor. Jobs were few, and typecasting was rampant. He changed his profession to electronics and started his own company for designing and installing home theatre systems in Oregon and Texas. He now lives in San Diego, California. Besides his business, Radames also shoots short films, surfs, and writes. Young Grasshopper found the peace to follow the path of his own desires.

BRIAN PART

(Born March 24, 1962)

Character: Carl Sanderson Edwards

Brian has stated that his appearances on *Little House* were "the most wonderful experiences anyone could ever have." The enjoyment of acting continued as he appeared in the movies *Max Dugan Returns* and *Return from Witch Mountain*. He also caught roles on popular series in the early 1980s. But he retired from his film career in 1983 and turned his talents to the music world. After a serious physical bout with a dislocated shoulder and the drugs used to control the pain, he now tours with bands, records CDs, and plays music with his wife, Melody. He is a man happily marching to his own beat.

KYLE RICHARDS

(Born January 11, 1969)
Character: Alicia Sanderson Edwards

Kyle was the third child adopted by the Edwards when her "reel" mother (Patricia Neal) died. Besides *Little House* work, Kyle appeared in *Escape to Witch Mountain* as the younger version of her real sister Kim, who appeared in the film as Tia Malone. After *Little House*, Kyle continued to work in films and TV but found most fame in her role as one of the cast members in *The Real Housewives of Beverly Hills*. Plying one of her other talents, Kyle wrote a memoir in 2011 titled *Life Is Not a Reality Show: Keeping It Real with the Housewife Who Does It All*. Kyle continues to do it all as wife to second husband Mauricio Umansky (a Beverly Hills luxury real estate broker), mother to their three daughters and daughter Farrah from her first husband, Guraish Aldjufrie, actress, and philanthropist. The family's charity of choice is Childrens Hospital Los Angeles, where they have donated over $100,000. Her prairie days behind her, Kyle opts for the very upscale suburban life.

PATRICK LABYORTEAUX

(Born July 22, 1965)

Character: Andrew "Andy" Garvey

Joining the *Little House* cast in 1977, Patrick is the real-life older, adopted brother of castmate Matthew Labyorteaux. Patrick has enjoyed a nice entertainment career with roles in TV, movies, and voice-over animation. He played the role of Bud Roberts on the TV series *Jag* from 1995 to 2005 which bled over to *Yes, Dear* and then the popular series *NCIS*. He and his wife, Tina Albanese, have a son and together they created the Nick at Nite sitcom *See Dad Run* starring Scott Baio. Patrick continues to find enjoyment in the business and satisfaction in the community through his and his brother's foundation, the Youth Rescue Fund.

BRENDA TURNBAUGH
WENDI TURNBAUGH

(Twins born on August 13, 1977)

Character: Grace Ingalls

Choosing identical twins on *Little House* to play the babies allowed the company to get more done during production days, as the young ones could only work a limited number of hours. Kent McCray, the producer of the show, had seen success with the Greenbush twins, so Brenda and Wendi, whose grandmother was friends with McCray, got the job as Grace, the youngest member of the Ingalls family, in 1978. In 1982 when the show was over, the twins did one commercial and retired from showbiz. Brenda, the older twin, secured her teaching credential for high school, but presently is tending to her two children and her husband, Adam. Wendi studied psychology at Biola University and is a web designer. She has been married to Joshua Lee since 1999. The twins enjoy their life away from the camera, but they are still connected by twenty miles of suburban road between them.

JASON BATEMAN

(Born January 14, 1969)

Character: James Cooper Ingalls

Jason held onto only one season of *Little House,* but the experience helped to springboard him to many roles on series in the 1980s and 1990s, including *Silver Spoons*, *It's Your Move*, and *Valerie*. He also guest-starred on many TV-movies during that time period. His sister, Justine Bateman, was also a child star and talented actress in *Family Ties*, among other shows. Jason admits that in the nineties he struggled with alcohol and drugs; he has stated, "It was like *Risky Business* for ten years." In the 2000s he got his wild feet tamed and back on the ground; he starred in one of his signature series, *Arrested Development,* and further developed his career by directing and producing. A successful adult actor, he continues his movie career in such fare as *Horrible Bosses* and *The Gift*. He also lends his voice to movies, such as *Zootopi*a, and the series *Growing Up Fisher*. He has been married since 2001 to Amanda, the daughter of Paul Anka, and they have two daughters. The thoroughly adult Jason is now a successful and grounded family man.

MISSY FRANCIS

(Born December 12, 1972)

Character: Cassandra Cooper Ingalls

As a two-season graduate of *Little House*, Missy went on to further graduate with a bachelor's degree in economics from Harvard University. Her 2012 book, *Diary of a Stage Mother's Daughter: A Memoir*, chronicles her life along with the "trials, tribulations, and joys" of having an overbearing mother. Sometimes a stage mother can prod her child to do wonderful things; sometime she can drive her away from fame and accomplishment. After her stint on *Little House*, Missy achieved accolades by appearing in other TV series and movies. The grown Melissa, however, found her true calling as a news journalist, now cohosting on Fox News's *Outnumbered* and starring on her own show for the Fox Business Network, *MONEY with Melissa Francis*. She has been married since 1997 to Wray Thorn and enjoys life with him and their two children. She has established her own secure *House*.

JENNIFER STEFFIN
MICHELLE STEFFIN

(Twins born on March 23, 1981)

Character: Rose Wilder

Twins again! This time the identical duo belongs to faux parents Laura and Almanzo Wilder. Their one-season experience as children on the series did not seem to appeal to the youthful pair, as they gave up their career shortly after appearing in *Little House* movie sequels and went on to excel in high school activities. Finance seemed more beckoning, and they now work their magic in accounting. Jennifer is in medical billing, and Michelle's number is up in Rancho Cucamonga, where she studied for a career in human resources after working as an auditor.

ALLISON BALSON

(Born November 19, 1969)
Character: Nancy Oleson

Allison, a smart cookie, first gathered together all her sweet ingredients as a child model. Securing commercials and then TV work, she had roles in *CHiPs* and *Quincy M.E.* before she hit the prairie. Graduating from Princeton University with a bachelor's degree followed by an MBA from Trinity College, University of Dublin, Ireland, she blends musical pastry today by writing songs and performing music. In 2012, she created a radio show that she produces and hosts called *Music Scene Live*—where singer/songwriters appear before a live audience. Her trail of musical notes is followed by aficionados worldwide. Alison and I, your author, will be appearing in a new movie, *Heaven with a Gun*, filming in 2016 under the banner of Brenrock Productions.

The Jeffersons

11 Seasons: 253 half-hour episodes

Network: CBS; Color

Debut: January 18, 1975 / Finale: July 2, 1985

This *All in the Family* spin-off saw the Bunkers' African-American neighbors movin' on up to a high-rise apartment building in Manhattan as the result of the Jeffersons' business success. During the first few weeks of its run, a number of CBS affiliates in the South refused to air the program due to the casting of a mixed-race couple, the Willises. Just as was the case for producer Norman Lear's other shows, however, what was once controversial became the norm, and *The Jeffersons* went on to become one of the longest-running sitcoms ever. The depiction of a wealthy black family was new to television, and while the series began as a topical romp, it became more of a softer domestic comedy as it entered the 1980s.

EBONIE SMITH

(Born September 16, 1978)

Character: Jessica Jefferson

Ebonie got her theatrical start on *The Jeffersons*, appearing on one season as the daughter of Jenny and Lionel and granddaughter of George and Isabel. The young actress expanded her career when she played in all four of the popular *Lethal Weapon* movies as one of Danny Glover's daughters. Interspersing these films were appearances as Penny Peyser on TV's *Family Matters* and roles in other TV series and popular movies. After gaining a fine arts degree in film production and Chinese language and culture, she is now a music composer a happily transitioned ex–child star.

One Day at a Time

9 Seasons: 209 episodes

Network: CBS; Color

Debut: December 16, 1975 / Finale: May 18, 1984

Another program developed by Norman Lear, *One Day at a Time,* was also the brainchild of Whitney Blake, former star of *Hazel* and mother to Meredith Baxter. It was another barrier-breaking concept show, this time about a woman newly divorced after twenty years of marriage who retakes her maiden name and moves into a small apartment with her two teenage daughters. Like other Lear programs, *One Day at a Time* often explored topics such as premarital sex, drug abuse, and other hot-button issues. As the series continued, all three of the original female cast members became married, and the show, like *My Three Sons* before it, morphed into a sitcom about extended families.

Mackenzie Phillips, Valerie Bertinelli, and Greg Evigan on the set of *One Day at a Time*.
CBS/Photofest

VALERIE BERTINELLI

(Born April 23, 1960)

Character: Barbara Cooper

Having secured an agent for her talented daughter, Valerie's mother took her on an audition for TV's *Apple Way,* and she booked her first job. After the pretty girl was cast in *One Day at a Time,* Valerie's successful road to fame really began, and she embraced it wholeheartedly. After an admitted but brief foray into the world of drugs and alcohol during the run of the series, Valerie turned that corner and stayed on a straight path to screen popularity. When the show ended, she continued acting in TV-movies and starred in two short-lived series, *Sydney* and *Cafe Americain.* Valerie successfully joined the cast of *Touched by an Angel* for fifty-nine episodes, as Gloria. Also well known for her appearances as a Jenny Craig spokesperson, the active entertainer wrote two books outlining her struggle and victory over weight gain: *Losing It: And Gaining My Life Back One Pound at a Time* and *Finding It: And Satisfying My Hunger for Life without Opening the Fridge.* Valerie starred in TV Land's original series *Hot in Cleveland* from 2010 to 2014. She divorced rocker Eddie Van Halen in 2007 after twenty-six years of marriage and is now happily married to financier Tom Vitale. She has one son, Wolfgang Van Halen, and a satisfying life as a successful ex–child star.

MACKENZIE PHILLIPS

(Born November 10, 1959)
Character: Julie Cooper

Mackenzie began her entertainment career early. With a father like John Phillips from the famous singing group *The Mamas and the Papas,* it was no wonder that she was encouraged to pursue a musical career. Mackenzie formed a band when she was just twelve years old, and a casting director saw her and cast her in the iconic film *American Graffiti*. Norman Lear saw her on an audition, and she was then cast in his new series *One Day at a Time*. In the third season of her long-running series, Mac was arrested for cocaine possession and public drunkenness. She was twice fired from the show and sent to rehab, but she kept relapsing. Even though Mackenzie acted in a few episodics and starred in the Disney series *So Weird* as Molly Phillips in 1999, she was still in the grip of addiction. In 2009 her autobiography, *High on Arrival: A Memoir,* was released, and she stated that her father had injected her with cocaine when she was just eleven years old. Mackenzie was cast in the reality show *Celebrity Rehab* in 2010. In 2011 I worked with Mac in the movie *Hercules Saves Christmas*, and she seemed to be over the more difficult times of her life. She is presently a drug-rehab counselor in Pasadena, California.

Family

5 Seasons: 86 episodes

Network: ABC; Color

Debut: March 9, 1976 / Finale: June 25, 1980

Family was an Aaron Spelling–produced weekly drama that attempted to depict the daily ups and downs of an average, middle-class Pasadena, California, family—with an emphasis on *drama*. The typical episode would explore how to overcome feelings of adolescent inadequacy or combatting the boredom of being a housewife.

KRISTY McNICHOL

(Born September 11, 1962)

Character: Letitia "Buddy" Lawrence

Kristy found her own way after being a successful child actor and teen idol. She left her series, *Empty Nest,* when she was diagnosed with bipolar disorder in 1992, returned for the final episode in 1995, and has not been on the screen since. She also came out as a lesbian in 2012 and has proclaimed that she hopes this admission will help others accept those who live a different way of life. The Emmy-winning actress starred in *Family* for four years, in big movies, and in celebrity-based reality shows. She and her brother Jimmy recorded an album, *Kristy and Jimmy McNichol,* and she used her musical talent on two of the Carpenters' Christmas specials. She is now making her own music teaching at a private school and composing her own life.

QUINN CUMMINGS

(Born August 13, 1967)

Character: Annie Cooper

Oscar-nominated Quinn (for her role in the movie *The Goodbye Girl*) had other jaunts into the TV-series realm before she landed the role of Annie, the orphan adopted by the Cooper family in season four. After the series was canceled, she played the daughter of Patty Duke in the short-lived TV show *Hail to the Chief* before she found that Hollywood wasn't hiring. After two years at UCLA, she sought jobs in the entertainment world as a casting agent, but found her true joy was in writing. Her first book emerged in 2009; it was called *Notes from the Underwire: Adventures from My Awkward and Lovely Life.* Finding success in the literary world, she then went on to publish *The Year of Learning Dangerously* in 2012. *Pet Sounds* came into being in 2013. Quinn now writes a popular blog and comments on her life, her daughter, Anneke, by partner Don DiPietro, and ex–child star experiences.

The New Mickey Mouse Club

2 Seasons: 130 half-hour episodes

Network: Syndicated; Color

Debut: January 17, 1977 / Finale: October 18, 1977

Mouseketeers have a special place in the annals of child acting. While each was a star in his or her own earned right, some broke out to become more famous child and adult stars. DVDs of this beloved show are due out in 2016. Here is a list of the 1970s Mouseketeers and where they are now. Enjoy.

BILLY "POP" ATTMORE

(Born March 19, 1965)

Born in West Germany, Billy "Pop" appeared in the Disney movie *Treasure of Matecumbe* before he joined the club. He stayed with acting until 1996, when he began to voice characters in the *Spider-Man* TV series. He and his wife, Lisa, whom he married in 2004, have a daughter who was born in 2007. William operates a cleaning business during the day and recently finished writing a book called *Broken Dreams*.

SCOTT CRAIG

(February 9, 1964–December 30, 2003)

Talented and musical Scott's primary TV career was centered on *The New Mickey Mouse Club,* following stints on commercials. From Los Angeles he moved to Las Vegas, where he owned and operated an artificial flower distributorship. He also played in his band at night called Scott and Sassy. He died of respiratory failure at the age of thirty-nine.

NITA DEE (DI GIAMPAOLO)

(Born August 6, 1966)

An experienced dancer by the time she won a spot on TV, Nita was one of the youngest of the mice. After the show was canceled, she continued to work in TV and had a role in a short-lived series titled *Upbeat Aesop.* But she has stated that it was difficult getting work beyond the Club and that her mother couldn't take her on interviews anymore. In a 2001 article she said, "I don't know if I would recommend show business for a child. It is very stressful." Her last part was in *Fantasy Island* in 1981. Her present role is wife, mother to four children, and resident of Long Beach, California.

MINDY FELDMAN

(Born July 4, 1968)

Mindy was the youngest of the group with little dancing or singing experience, but she did have extensive acting credits. She had appeared in commercials and acting roles on TV. After the show she had a couple of parts in films, but she then retired from the business. In the 1990s Mindy worked for CMI Marketing and now is raising her children and enjoying life. She did not have quite as an illustrious career as her younger brother, Corey.

ANGEL FLOREZ

(August 13, 1963—August 25, 1995)

Triple-threat entertainer Florez enjoyed his work on *The Mickey Mouse Club*, according to his parents. The role of Mouseketeer was Angel's only professional work before he left the business. He died of AIDs and now is flying as an angel around heavenly spires.

ALLISON FONTE

(Born June 6, 1964)

The mice were quite talented. Allison could sing, dance, write poetry, and do gymnastics! But when the show ended, Allison's heady ideas took over. She graduated from Stanford University, headed east to cofound a design company for commercial spaces, Pompeii AD, and then opened a public-relations firm in 2000. Now back in Northern California she continues her public-relations acumen and enjoys the balmy weather of the San Francisco Bay Area.

SHAWNTE NORTHCUTTE

(Born February 25, 1965)

Shawnte graduated from the stage of Disneyland as a Mouseketeer to a TV-screen mouse on the Club. Holding the title of Miss Pre-teen California from 1975 to 1976, she also had aspirations of being a lawyer. But she found real estate more to her liking and works as an appraiser in Los Angeles.

KELLY PARSONS

(Born January 23, 1964)

The beautiful Kelly, who was crowned Our Little Miss in 1975, gave up her duties as pageant royalty to concentrate on her musical and tap duties as a Mouseketeer. However, even though she didn't appear for Our Little Miss, she did keep the title and a $2,000 college scholarship. After the series and a few more appearances on TV shows, she resumed her pageant career and was named Miss California USA in 1986. Kelly went on to be fourth runner-up in the thirty-fifth annual Miss USA contest and then ended her quests for tiaras. She is no longer in show business but occasionally attends Mouseketeer reunions.

JULIE PIEKARSKI

(Born January 2, 1964)

Over twenty-five trophies won in talent contests in St. Louis, Missouri, lined Julie's shelf before she was selected to be one of the twelve talented Mouseketeers in the Club. She enjoyed working, and so she continued acting when the show was over. She appeared in seventeen episodes of the *Facts of Life* with her Club pal Lisa Whelchel. After appearing in more TV fare, Julie went to UCLA and graduated with a degree in communications. While trying out her degree as an entertainment reporter for KLPR-TV from 1986 to 1988, she met and married her husband, dentist John Probst. The couple and their three children live in St Louis. You *can* go home again.

TODD TURQUAND

(Born December 14, 1964)

Todd was one of the most experienced children on-screen of all the mice when he was selected to join the Club. He had starred for one season as the stepson of Valerie Harper on the TV series *Rhoda* and guested on many TV episodics. When the Club was canceled, Todd did a few more acting jobs but found, after attending the University of Southern California, that he might be able to conquer the business world. After working in sales for Europa Watch Company, he became its president and then opened his own business, Topshelf Marketing. Some child stars can do almost anything they put their mind and spirit to.

LISA WHELCHEL

(Born May 29, 1963)

Lisa is of one of the child star success stories. Determination has always been part of her character, and she used that perseverance to gain an audition for *The New Mickey Mouse Club,* which led her to her starring role as Blair Warner in the long-running series *Facts of Life*. She was a Grammy Award nominee for Best Inspirational Performance for her album *All Because of You*. Married for twenty-three years to Steven Cauble, they have three children, whom Lisa homeschooled in her native state of Texas. Now divorced, she made a splash as second-place winner on *Survivor: Philippines* in 2012. Lisa has written ten books primarily focused on motherhood and how to raise children with spirit and guidance. Her determination has led her to follow her path as a Christian and as a survivor of ex–child-star syndrome.

CURTIS WONG

(Born August 23, 1962)

Another singer and dancer who had won local talent shows in his Vancouver, British Columbia, hometown, Curtis had been cast in two commercials before he was selected as the last and the oldest of the mice. He, like other members of the Club, found it hard going when the two-season show was canceled. But he did find some use for his karate expertise in an episode of TV's *Diff'rent Strokes,* and he was able to put that skill to further use. He attends reunions of the Club and reminisces with the other ex–child actors about the good times they had when they were singing, dancing, and cavorting—while their talented lights shined brightest.

Eight Is Enough

5 Seasons: 112 episodes

Network: ABC; Color

Debut: March 15, 1977 / Finale: May 25, 1981

Eight Is Enough was an hour-long dramedy, complete with laugh track, that debuted midseason in 1976–77 and was an instant hit. The series centered on Sacramento columnist Tom Bradford (Dick Van Patten) and his family of eight children, ranging in age from eight to mid-twenties. Tragedy befell the just-launched show when its matriarch, Diana Hyland, suddenly died of cancer only a few episodes into the first season. Betty Buckley was brought in for year two, and she quickly married the widowed Bradford. Good thing, too—with those kids, Tom needed all the help he could get!

The cast of *Eight Is Enough*. Shown clockwise from center: Dick Van Patten, Adam Rich, Lani O'Grady, Susan Richardson, Dianne Kay, Lauri Walters, Connie (Newton) Needham, Willie Aames, Michael Thoma.

ABC/Photofest

GRANT GOODEVE

(Born July 6, 1952)
Character: David Bradford

Grant, the oldest Bradford son, took over the role of David that Mark Hamill had originated in the pilot when Mark was injured in a car accident and unable to proceed. At the start of his career Grant appeared on *One Life to Live* but decided to concentrate on his studies and left acting to attend and then graduate from Ithaca College. He restarted his career with roles in TV-movies and shows in Los Angeles before he claimed the role of David. He married Deborah Lynn Ketcham in 1978 and continued acting in Los Angeles on such shows as *TJ Hooker, The Love Boat,* and *Dynasty.* In 1989 he moved his family, which consisted of three children, to Washington State, where he captured a recurring role in the TV series *Northern Exposure.* He has been host of *Northwest Backroad*s for seventeen years, as of 2015. He intersperses this task with acting in industrials, commercials, and onstage. Grant splits his time between homes in Washington, Georgia, and California. I knew Grant when he was on *Eight.* He was a very grounded and personable actor who, while not a young child star when he began his career, was a successful survivor of series cancellation.

LANI O'GRADY

(October 2, 1954–September 25, 2001)
Character: Mary Bradford

Sister of Don Grady from *My Three Sons* and daughter of talent agent Mary Grady, Lani had a boost up to find success in a show business career. However, she was derailed by drug addiction when she was misdiagnosed on *Eight* and given Xanax and a veritable cocktail of prescription antianxiety drugs. After the show was canceled, she appeared on the *Eight Is Enough* reunion shows but retired in 1999; her last screen appearance was a role on *Days of Our Lives*. She then went to work for her mom, but she died of an apparent overdose of Vicodin and Prozac. She is quoted as saying in 1994, "I have a real hard time with people who have been successful in this business as young children . . . and [as adults] and, yeah, Hollywood is not a user-friendly place."

LAURIE WALTERS

(Born January 8, 1947)
Character: Joanie Bradford

Laurie, while technically not a child star, acted in the Bradford family of child stars and was hired as the third eldest in the clan. She was actually six months older than Betty Buckley, who played her stepmother in the show, and dated Grant Goodeve, her "reel" brother before he was married. She began her professional career in her twenties as the character of Sheila Grove in the film *The Harrad Experiment*. After the series, Laurie continued acting, but her last on-screen performance was in 1999. As Laurie Walters Slade, she is a dedicated environmentalist working with the TreePeople. She also is involved with Ironweed Films, which distributes indie documentaries and short films. Laurie has been married to John Slade since 1999.

SUSAN RICHARDSON

(Born March 11, 1952)
Character: Susan Bradford

Pretty Susan Richardson first wrote on the theatrical wall in the movie *American Graffiti*. She went on to guest star in episodics before she landed the part of the fourth oldest child in the Bradford household. When the show was canceled, Susan found it difficult finding roles—a familiar plight of characters on TV series. Her search for roles was not helped when she claimed in 1987 that she had been kidnapped and almost murdered by North Korean filmmakers. The accuracy of this claim has still not been resolved. She suffered a nervous breakdown in 1999 and moved back to her home state of Pennsylvania, where she went to work as a caregiver at a retirement home. Susan reported in an interview in 2013 that she was suffering from "devastating" health problems. She is living with diabetes and has had several ministrokes. Digestive problems have caused her weight to plummet. She lives in a trailer and says, "There's always something wrong with it. I desperately need a new trailer, but I can't afford it." Hers is a sad tale not unknown to ex–child stars. Eight wasn't enough for sweet Susan.

DIANNE KAY

(Born March 29, 1954)
Character: Nancy Bradford

Like Grant, Dianne won a role in *Eight* when the producers decided to replace the girl originally cast, Kimberly Beck. When the show was canceled, Dianne went on to guest star in episodics such as *Jake and the Fat Man* and *Hangin' with Mr. Cooper*. Her last screen appearance was in *Diagnosis Murder* in 1999. She presently is a full-time mom and lives in Los Angeles with her husband and child. Eight was enough for Dianne.

CONNIE NEEDHAM

(Born December 5, 1959)
Character: Elizabeth Bradford

Originally billed as Connie Newton, this trained ballet dancer pirouetted her way into the cast and the hearts of the audience of *Eight*. When the show ended, she obtained a few parts, but she retired from the TV business in 1995; her last role was in an episode of the television series *Ellen*. Connie and her ex-husband, David, the son of director/producer Hal Needham, have two daughters, Kim and Taylor. In 2009, Connie was diagnosed with and treated for ovarian cancer. Happily, she is now cancer-free and teaching dancing in Rancho Santa Margarita, California, at Dance Dynamics. Besides training, the mission of the studio is to present positive role models that the children they teach can look up to and respect.

WILLIE AAMES

(Born July 15, 1960)
Character: Tommy Bradford

Willie had a long list of credits to his theatrical name before he landed the role of Tommy, including the series *The Courtship of Eddie's Father* as Harold O'Brien,

The Swiss Family Robinson as Fred Robinson, and *Family* as TJ Latimer. Unlike the experience of some of the other child stars, when *Eight* was canceled, he found work in other TV shows and even a series, *Charles in Charge,* where he played the part of Buddy Lembeck. But addiction to drugs and alcohol stopped his flow of roles, and he partially quit the entertainment world to accept work as a cruise director for five years. When he returned to the TV realm clean and sober, he became Bibleman in the series of the same name, fighting evil in the guise of an armored superhero. In 2008 he went bankrupt, studied business, and is now living in Kansas as a financial advisor.

ADAM RICH

(Born October 12, 1968)

Character: Nicholas Bradford

Adam Rich has had a tumultuous time in showbiz. He started his career at the age of eight in *The Six Million Dollar Man*. But he started smoking marijuana, it has been revealed, at the age of fourteen and then dropped out of high school at seventeen. The attraction of drugs caused him much trouble, as he almost died of a Valium overdose in 1989. In 2003 he was arrested for driving under the influence and was in rehab three times. Despite all these angst-creating moments, the youngest of the Bradford children, who was adored for his personality and bowl haircut, did work in the industry when the series was canceled. Shows such as *Code Red* and *Silver Spoons* were recipients of his talents, and he shared voice-over duties with Willie Ames in TV's animated series *Dungeons and Dragons*. Still attracted to drugs and show business, he is out and about pitching scripts to the powers that be with his six-million-dollar ideas.

RALPH MACCHIO

(Born November 4, 1961)

Character: Jeremy Andretti

Not one of the original Bradford clan, Ralph came to the family in the final season as Abby's orphaned nephew. According to some sources, the adoption of Jeremy was to help the flagging ratings and to add some youth appeal, but the addition couldn't help and the show was canceled. Ralph had no trouble staying in the public light after the show, as he became a star in *The Karate Kid* franchise. He did have some problems breaking the martial-arts image, but he has remained steadily working in the business with such films as *Crossroads, My Cousin Vinny,* and *The Outsiders*. On TV he is known for his role in *Ugly Betty* and for competing in *Dancing with the Stars*. Ralph has been married since 1987 to Phyllis Fierro and they have two children. A life of an actor has its ups and downs. What rates high on an angst list is losing a job. Actors are constantly losing jobs, looking for jobs, getting them, and then losing them again. You've got to be tough and learn life skills to deal with such insecure employment. As Ralph has said, "The truth is you have a much richer life if you somehow lead one that you can hold together." Good advice for the rest of the family in the Bradford household and child stars everywhere.

Battlestar Galactica

1 Season: 24 episodes

Network: ABC; Color

Debut: September 17, 1978 / Finale: April 29, 1979

The *Star Wars* craze spawned this super-high-tech/high-concept and very expensive science-fiction drama in the fall of 1978. Debuting with a three-hour pilot episode, the show was named for the final battlestar of a civilization of humans fleeing from hostile machines who have taken over humanity on the *Galactica*'s planet. Their destination? A place called Earth. Regrettably, slick effects and flashy laser fights don't help weak stories and a cast lacking chemistry, and the series folded after only one season.

Noah Hathaway and Richard Hatch in *Battlestar Galactica*, c. 1978–79.
ABC/Photofest

NOAH HATHAWAY

(Born November 13, 1971)

Character: Boxey

Noah began his career at just three years old in commercials—having a father who is an actor and music editor always helps to jump-start entry into the screen world. When Noah was seven, he landed his role in *Battlestar*, and even though the series only lasted one year, he was at the beginning of the sci-fi cult era. Noah also gained recognition in 1984 for his part as the young hero Atreyu in the now-classic film *The NeverEnding Story*. Later, he taught jazz and street dancing until an injury curtailed this activity, and he became a production coordinator. Presently he designs and rides customized motorcycles and is hoping to open his own shop along with, of course, acting jobs interspersed. He and his wife, galactic beauty Sameerah, have two sons.

Mrs. Columbo / Kate Loves a Mystery

2 Seasons: 13 episodes

Network: NBC; Color

Debut: February 26, 1979 / Finale: March 19, 1980

Desperately seeking ratings success anywhere, NBC mined the Columbo franchise for this spin-off of sorts with an ad campaign that proclaimed, "Yes, there really *is* a Mrs. Columbo!" Mrs. Columbo was the often-mentioned but never-seen spouse of the popular TV detective. After the original run of *Columbo* ended in 1978, NBC decided to demonstrate how the Columbo household ran when the famous lieutenant was on a case. Put simply, Mrs. Columbo was an early version of *Murder, She Wrote*. Rumor has it that the show was originally designed for Jean Stapleton, who was exiting *All in the Family*, but NBC turned it into a vehicle for the young Kate Mulgrew instead. Regrettably, while the show was charming, the adventures of a San Fernando Valley housewife who stumbles upon murders did not keep the interest of the public.

LILI HAYDN

(Born December 25, 1971)

Character: Jenny Columbo

Although Lili was just a child star for one season on *Mrs. Columbo,* she was a child prodigy at the violin, which she continues to play until this day. Her passion brought her fame as a musician. She was an honorary member of George Clinton's band, and George nicknamed her the "Jimi Hendrix of the Violin." Lili suffered brain damage in 2009 that she traced to toxic poisoning, but she claims that music helped rid her of the toxins. She is now widely heralded as a rock violinist, vocalist, and recording artist. An upbringing by very progressive-thinking parents led Lili to be creative and manipulate her own strings.

Diff'rent Strokes

8 Seasons: 189 episodes

Network: NBC (1978–85); ABC (1985–86); Color

Debut: November 3, 1978 / Finale: March 7, 1986

Introducing . . . the series that saved a network—seriously. *Diff'rent Strokes* debuted late in the fall of 1978 and starred a clever, diminutive child who had been charming audiences on shows such as *Good Times* and *The Jeffersons*. America fell in love with Gary Coleman instantly, and this series was NBC's only entry in the top thirty programs of all networks some weeks. The premise was simple: A rich, white millionaire promises to care for the children of his dying African-American maid, and he moves two young boys from Harlem into his midtown Manhattan town house. The plots were predictable and the stories often syrupy sweet, but when Coleman was on his game, it was hilarious.

The children of *Diff'rent Strokes*. Shown from left: Gary Coleman, Todd Bridges, Dana Plato.
NBC/Photofest

GARY COLEMAN

(February 8, 1968–May 28, 2010)

Character: Arnold Jackson Drummond

The poster child for ex–child stars, tiny Gary Coleman fought lawyers, his adoptive parents, and the Hollywood way before he died of a brain hemorrhage caused by a fall down the stairs of his home in Utah, after he had been weakened by heart surgery months earlier. Initially discovered by a talent agent from Norman Lear's production company in Chicago, where Gary was delighting audiences with his vivacious comedic takes in commercials, Gary and his family moved to Los Angeles, where he appeared on *The Jeffersons* and other Norman Lear shows before he was given his own series. TV fans loved the adorable cherub's effervescence and his tag line, "Whatchoo talkin' 'bout, Willis?", kept the show on the air for eight seasons.

Then it was over. And Gary was seventeen. No longer the cute little boy, he found obtaining roles difficult; his mother and father, posing as managers, had spent most of the alleged $18 million dollars Gary had earned during his series reign (he reportedly was making $70,000 per episode) and his work on TV-movies and films. By suing his parents, he did redeem $1,265,000 of what was due him, but it was quickly used up to pay for his medical bills (he had to have continued dialysis, as he had only one, weak, kidney), legal fees, and other expenses.

Gary declared bankruptcy in 1999, ran, as a stunt, for governor of California, worked as a security guard, and finally fled to Utah. His ex-wife, Shannon Price, who was married to Gary for two years and who had accused him of domestic violence, was at the house, which was filled with toy trains, when he suffered his fatal fall. As Gary stated, "I parody myself every chance I get. I try to make fun of myself and let people know that I'm a human being, and these things that have happened to me are real. I'm not some cartoon who exists and suddenly doesn't exist."

Dealing with the pinnacle of success and recognition by millions and then being dropped to the nadir would give anyone pause, but for a child to try to adjust without an adequate support system was too much. Gary would have benefited from anger management, that is, a way in to the root of his anger—to the psychologically debilitating stance of a person who was adored then ignored. The experience created bitterness and aggression in him against the beast of Hollywood, its audiences, and even himself.

TODD BRIDGES

(Born May 27, 1965)
Character: Willis Drummond

Athletic and talented Todd began his show business career at six years old. After appearing in a Jell-O ad, he hawked products on more than fifty commercials. One of the first modern black successful child actors, he appeared as a semi-regular on *The Waltons* and went on to hone his acting chops with a regular part on *Fish* before he was chosen to cross the divide into Norman Lear's racially mixed and now iconic *Diff'rent Strokes*. He also gained critical acclaim on *Roots* and other TV specials and shows.

When the series ended, so did Todd's belief in himself. He couldn't get roles, he claims, because of typecasting. He could get drugs, which soothed his bitterness but did not control his anger about former producers and casting directors not hiring him. He got into trouble with the law numerous times and was struggling. Then he found an answer—God came into his life. He got off drugs and established a meaningful career in acting, directing, producing, and giving motivational speeches. In his 2008 book, *Killing Willis: From Diff'rent Strokes to Mean Streets to the Life I Always Wanted*, he writes how he was able to rid himself of his series persona to establish his true identity and find satisfaction. He and his wife, Dori, married in 1998 and have two children, one from a previous relationship. To quote Todd, "Stick with God."

DANA PLATO

(November 7, 1964–May 8, 1999)
Character: Kimberly Drummond

Dana completes the triumvirate of child stars in *Strokes* who were plagued with doubt, discouragement, and tribulation in their struggles to succeed when the limelight faded. Dana, born to an unwed teenage mother and then adopted by the Platos, worked in a string of commercials before landing her first TV role in *The Six Million Dollar Man*. Also an accomplished ice skater, her hopes of being a young professional in that field were curtailed when she was cast in *Strokes*. Reports are that she was taking drugs and drinking while she was on the series and experienced an overdose of Diazepam when she was fourteen.

Dana continued with substance abuse until she became pregnant at nineteen and was married in 1984. The producers of *Strokes* fired her; they contended that a pregnant Kimberly did not fit the narrative of the show. After her son, Tyler, was born, she returned to appear in some of the episodes from 1986 to 1988. When the show was canceled she tried, like the other ex–child stars in the series, to change people's perception of her, and she looked for serious parts, but Hollywood was not buying. To try to escape her wholesome image, she posed nude for *Playboy* and appeared in soft porn and in X-rated films. Experiencing financial troubles—she reported that her accountant had stolen from her—Dana moved to Las Vegas. Desperate for money, she worked for a dry cleaner and then robbed a video store.

Singer Wayne Newton came to her rescue and posted her $13,000 bail but was unable to help with her other troubles. Dana still thought she could find acting roles, hired manager Robert Menchaca, and lived with him in a motor home in Florida. On a cross-country trek they stopped in Moore, Oklahoma, to pay a Mother's Day visit to his parents. Dana went to their Winnebago, which was parked near the Menchaca home, and overdosed on prescription drugs Soma and Lortab. The coroner stated that Dana's overdose was intentional and ruled her death a suicide. Her son, Tyler, died eleven years later of a self-inflicted shot to the head at the age of twenty-five.

Tragic, sad, and . . . avoidable? The treatise at the end of this book points to an approach that might help child stars avoid some of the pitfalls and dangers of show business; it's a compilation of ways to alleviate some of the anxiety, stress, and financial troubles that can be associated with falling out of the limelight. We want our national treasures to be able to live lives free of desperation, anger, and lowered self-esteem—successful lives of satisfaction of their own making.

Hello, Larry

2 Seasons: 38 episodes

Network: NBC; Color

Debut: January 26, 1979 / Finale: April 30, 1980

NBC first started mining *Diff'rent Strokes* early in 1979 with this "related" show about a radio talk-show host in Portland, Oregon, raising his two teenage daughters alone. Host Larry Alder was Mr. Drummond's college friend, and the shows would often cross over. Not often enough, it would seem: Cast changes and format revisions couldn't save this sinking ship.

KRISTA ERRICKSON

(Born May 8, 1964)
Character: Diane Alder

As granddaughter of award-winning stage set designer Jo Mielziner and goddaughter to Elia Kazan, it is no wonder that Krista would wander into show business. However, her heart and mind were elsewhere, as she became a journalist, documentarian, and author. After the failed *Hello, Larry* show, she gave a breakthrough movie performance in *Little Darlings* and appeared in another critically acclaimed movie, *Mortal Passions*. Graduating from college with a BS in political science, she put her degree to work by becoming a news journalist for *RadioTelevisioneItalia* and then became a radio and TV host for RAI. She was the first female reporter to interview Sheikh Sayyid Hassan Nasrallah for her documentary *Inside the Hezbollah* (2001), and she has won awards for her programs. She was married once, to Piero di Pasquale, and divorced in 2004. She continues her crusades and journalistic career, definitely marching to the beat of her own political drum.

KIM RICHARDS

(Born September 19, 1964)
Character: Ruthie Alder

Kim's sisters and relatives are almost as interesting as her child star career. She is the older sister of Kyle Richards (*Little House on the Prairie*), half-sister of Kathy

Hilton, and aunt of Nicky Hilton, Barron Hilton, Conrad Hilton, and Paris Hilton. Kim was in many commercials before she appeared on *Nanny and the Professor,* and she gained recurring parts on *James at Sixteen* and guest spots on other shows. She is quite memorable in *Escape to Witch Mountain* and the sequel *Return to Witch Mountain* as the psychic alien girl. Married twice, she took a hiatus from acting for ten years to raise her four children before returning to the screen for the movie *Black Snake Moon,* and she is now appearing in the controversial reality series *Real Housewives of Beverly Hills.* She is a real ex–child star who went through trials of transition and substance abuse for all to see but now is still recovering for all to see.

The Facts of Life

9 Seasons: 209 episodes

Network: NBC; Color

Debut: August 24, 1979 / Finale: May 7, 1988

NBC was in a historic ratings spiral downward by the spring of 1979, with only *Diff'rent Strokes* counting as a sure-fire hit. Years before Bill Cosby would revive the Peacock Network's fortunes and the sitcom format, the network decided a spin-off of the Drummond family maid, Mrs. Garrett, would provide a possible hit. Initially serving as a temporary housemother at an upscale all-girls school, Mrs. Garrett was eventually promoted to full-time status and a full-time series. *The Facts of Life* had a very rocky start—the cast was too large, the laughs were too few, and there seemed to be no direction. Enter Nancy McKeon as motorbike-riding Jo in Season 2 to stir up conflict, and the show became one of NBC's longest-running hits.

Kim Fields, former cast member of *The Facts of Life*, 2011.
Dr. Duru

LISA WHELCHEL

(Born May 29, 1963)

Character: Blair Warner

Lisa is of one of the child star success stories. Please see her bio under *The Mickey Mouse Club* heading. Determination has always been part of her character, and she used that perseverance to gain an audition for *The New Mickey Mouse Club,* which led her to her starring role as Blair Warner in the long-running *Facts of Life.* She was a Grammy Award nominee for Best Inspirational Performance for her album *All Because of You.* Married for twenty-three years to Steven Cauble, they have three children, whom Lisa homeschooled in her native state of Texas. Now divorced, she made a splash as second-place winner on *Survivor: Philippines* in 2012. Lisa has written ten books primarily focused on motherhood and how to raise children with spirit and guidance. Her determination has led her to follow her path as a Christian and as a survivor of ex–child-star syndrome.

KIM FIELDS

(Born May 12, 1969)

Character: Tootie Ramsey

Getting her theatrical feet wet in sitcoms such as *Mork and Mindy* and *Good Times,* Kim was just nine years old when hired to portray 'tween (twelve-year-old) Tootie. Tiny Tootie wore roller skates in some of the first season's scenes to help her height differential, but then was left on her own to grow and prosper in the series. When the show's plug was pulled, she attended Pepperdine University and secured a degree in telecommunications. She said in an interview with the *LA Times,* "I needed to learn how to do something else, so I wouldn't be twenty years old and sitting around waiting for my agent to call. I would have gone crazy sitting in my apartment doing that. I learned how to direct and produce." And she did direct and produce through her own company, Victory Entertainment, but also continued to act. Especially noteworthy was her part in the series *Living Single* (1993–98), where she appeared opposite Queen Latifah. Kim is married to Christopher Morgan, and they have two children. Kim not only made the transition from ex–child star, but wisely hedged her bets with a quality education and a desired degree in a "field" that she loves. It was announced in August of 2015 that Kim will be joining the cast of *The Real Housewives of Atlanta*.

MINDY COHN

(Born May 20, 1966)
Character: Natalie Green

Thirteen-year-old theatrical neophyte Mindy Cohn dove headfirst into the series swim with her role as Natalie after being chosen from producers viewing her at the private school she was attending. Acting in the series for its entire run, when that "pool" emptied, she got into the swim again by voicing Velma in the long-running *Scooby-Doo* animated franchise. She has also appeared on camera in various roles on TV shows and in independent films. Graduating with a degree in anthropology/ sociology from Loyola Marymount University, she smilingly said in a *Huffington Post* entry in 2013 that she is "freakishly well adjusted, with a life that's filled with love, collaboration, inspiration, humor, and adventure." Those are some nice words coming from an ex–child star!

NANCY McKEON

(Born April 4, 1966)

Character: Jo Polniaczek

Nancy came into *Facts* in the second season, but she had entered show business at two years old, modeling diapers. When her family followed her brother Philip from New York to Los Angeles, where he had garnered the role of Tommy Hyatt on the series *Alice*, Nancy also began working in TV. With shows such as *Starsky and Hutch* and *Fantasy Island* under her acting belt, she was ready to star in eight seasons of *Facts*. When the show ended, she continued to work on episodics and gained the lead in the series *Can't Hurry Love* and then the drama series *The Division*. She has been married to Marc Andrus, a cameraman/key grip, since 2003 and is enjoying her family life with their two children.

THE 1980s

Gimme a Break!

6 Seasons: 137 episodes

Network: NBC; Color

Debut: October 29, 1981 / Finale: May 12, 1987

The original premise of this show was the conflict between a widowed police chief struggling to raise his three daughters and his African-American housekeeper, Nell, who had a more liberal style of parenting. The chemistry was perfect between the stars, but when male lead Dolph Sweet passed away midway through the series, the show never recovered.

The cast of *Gimme a Break!* shown clockwise from left: Nell Carter, Lauri Hendler, Kari Michaelsen, Dolph Sweet, Lara Jill Miller.

KARI MICHAELSEN

(Born November 3, 1961)

Character: Katie Kanisky

As a "backstage baby"—her parents were professional entertainers—Kari learned the theatrical ropes early and made her debut at the age of five in an off-Broadway production of *Gypsy*. When her family moved to Los Angeles, she headed to Beverly Hills High School and then was accepted at UCLA. Kari was aspiring to a degree in psychology when she was chosen to star in *Gimme*. Let go after the beginning of the sixth and final season due to a format change, she returned to college and studied marketing, business, and promotion. She was married, is divorced, and has one child. Kari now tours the country presenting motivational speeches and encouraging others to follow their own paths.

LAURI HENDLER

(Born April 22, 1965)

Character: Julie Kanisky

Lauri is an ex–baby actor, appearing in her first professional role at eight months in a print ad. She first appeared in an on-camera commercial at eight years old, after which she started working steadily in TV and movies. Lauri's breakthrough role came with *Gimme*. After her role on the series wrapped, she moved to New York to formally study acting then returned to Los Angeles to put some of those lessons to work. After guest appearances on episodics and a TV pilot,

Lauri decided to change direction and developed a voice-over career. Sometimes you can lose heart when you know you are just right for certain on-camera roles but you repeatedly do not get them. Voice-over has more flexibility, belies typecasting, and pays very well. Lauri continues to work in this field with commercials and animation, but she occasionally does on-camera stints. She is married and is said to be raising fruit in her large orchard. It's comforting to reap a continuous bounty.

LARA JILL MILLER

(Born April 20, 1967)

Character: Samantha "Sam" Kanisky

Lara is an example of what a talented child can go on to accomplish in life. Prancing onto the Broadway stage as a child in a revival of *The Music Man* with Dick van Dyke, she then tap-danced onto *Gimme*. Intelligent Lara was determined to go to college and persevered to not only attain her bachelor's degree in politics and French but also a Juris Doctor from Fordham University School of Law. She passed the bar in three states, New York, New Jersey, and Pennsylvania—that's some insurance policy. Her heart always in acting, she played Dorothy in *The Wizard of Oz* on her return to Los Angeles and costarred with Annette Bening and John Goodman, among many other stellar actors, in NPR's magical version. Lara then developed an excellent voice-over career with starring roles in *Henry Hugglemonster, Curious George,* and *Doc McStuffins,* among others. It is wonderful to be able to write your own contracts.

JOEY LAWRENCE

(Born April 20, 1976)

Character: Joey Donovan

As a successful ex–child star, Joey has been following his acting and singing passions ever since he crunched his first bite of a Crackerjack when he was five. Appearing on *Gimme a Break* in the third season, Joey became the foster son of Nell Carter and "Chief" Kanisky, much to the delight of the fans of the show. After that show, he snagged another winning TV series, *Blossom,* in which he starred for five years. Sometimes you can't keep a good talent down, and Joey rose yet again to the challenge of a series in *Brotherly Love,* where he shared thespian duties with his real-life older brothers Matthew and Andrew. A couple of other short-lived series, *American Dreams* and *Run of the House,* followed before he struck TV series gold again with *Melissa and Joey* in 2010, which had a five-year run. He continues his passion for music and, besides having toured with a successful album, he sings elsewhere and has composed music for *Brotherly Love* and *Melissa and Joey.* He is married, has two children, and is a very active and seemingly well-adjusted ex–child star.

Family Ties

7 Seasons: 168 episodes

Network: NBC; Color

Debut: September 22, 1982 / Finale: May 14, 1989

NBC began climbing out of the ratings cellar with this domestic sitcom that launched the career of 1980s teen superstar Michael J. Fox. It was the Reagan era, and this series derived conflict from hippie-generation parents trying to impose their liberal views on their conservative, preppy, Reagan-loving teenagers.

MICHAEL J. FOX

(Born June 9, 1961)

Character: Alex Keaton

Award-winning Canadian actor Michael J. Fox has had his trials, but through perseverance and a positive attitude, he has found a path through life that is an

Michael J. Fox at the thirty-ninth
Emmy Awards in September 1987.
Alan Light

inspiration to many. Gaining early recognition as a fifteen-year-old playing ten-year-old Jamie in the British Columbian series *Leo and Me*, he followed this work with a move to Los Angeles with his family. He was struggling to attract acting roles until he landed the part of Alex, one that Matthew Broderick had turned down. During the phenomenal success of *Family Ties*, he was also cast in the first of what became the *Back to the Future* trilogy, replacing Eric Stoltz, who had begun filming the movie. Michael continued his successful film career with starring roles in *Teen Wolf, Light of Day,* and *Casualties of War,* among others.

In 1991 while shooting *Doc Hollywood,* Michael learned of his debilitating Parkinson's disease. He took a hiatus from on-camera work and started drinking heavily, but he filled his creative need with starring roles in animated films before landing another successful sitcom, *Spin City*. Not one to look down on his tribulations, Michael wrote the books *Lucky Man: A Memoir, Always Looking Up: The Adventures of an Incurable Optimist,* and in 2010, *A Funny Thing Happened on the Way to the Future: Twists and Lessons Learned*. Coming to grips with his disease, he started the Michael J. Fox Foundation to help research Parkinson's and to find a way to make significant contributions to end or at least ameliorate the symptoms of the disease.

Michael had not graduated high school as a youth, but he was presented with an honorary diploma. Realizing the importance of education, he later obtained his GED. He is reported to have forbidden his kids to quit high school for Hollywood. He also is quoted as having said in 2014, "Look at the choices you have, not at the choices that have been taken away from you. In them, there are whole worlds of strength and new ways to look at things."

JUSTINE BATEMAN

(Born February 19, 1966)
Character: Mallory Keaton

Continuing a go-getter attitude after *Family Ties*, which was Justine's first gig, she appeared in episodics, starred opposite Julia Roberts in the memorable movie *Satisfaction,* and then started a clothing line in 2000 and managed it until 2003. Marrying well to real estate developer Mark Fluent, she had two children and then thought it was time to get down to something she found very important besides her family: the marriage of technology to the entertainment industry. To help her understand the nuances and daily changes of the fast-paced high-tech world, she enrolled at UCLA and in 2015 was in her junior year at the university. Her major is digital management and computer science, and she has a Tumblr page where she writes about her college life. Justine definitely was able to jump the ex–child star shark.

TINA YOTHERS

(Born May 5, 1973)

Character: Jennifer Keaton

Tina was a veteran screen presence when she snagged the role of Jennifer after appearances in commercials, the TV-movie *Cherokee Trail,* and the film *Shoot the Moon.* After the series, she took a breather and blew life into a singing career with her brother Cory's band called Jaded. She wrote a book in 1987 called *Being Your Best: Tina Yothers' Guide for Girls.* Trying to follow her own dictum she participated in the reality shows *Celebrity Fit Club* and *What Not to Wear.* Presently she is living with her electrician husband, whom she married in 2002, and their two children. She enjoys swimming and playing hockey, strong diversions from the unsettling world of show business.

BRIAN BONSALL

(Born December 3, 1981)
Character: Andy Keaton

Adorable child actor Brian joined the Keaton household in the sixth season when he was just five years old. When the series ended, he acted in some TV-movies, starred in the controversial film *Mikey,* as a boy who kills people, and then appeared intermittently as Alexander Rozhenko, son of Worf, in *Star Trek: The Next Generation.* In 1995 he moved to Colorado with his mother and stepfather, dropped out of high school, and formed the band Late Bloomers. He has stated that music is his passion, as it seems are his tattoos and piercings. As of 2015, he sings and plays guitar in the acoustic duo Bootjack & Bonz, has been arrested for DUI, assault, and drugs, but has settled comfortably into the Colorado scene and vowed never to go back to acting. He really is an X–child star.

Silver Spoons

5 Seasons: 116 episodes

Network: NBC; Color

Debut: September 25, 1982 / Finale: March 4, 1987

Like *Family Ties*, *Silver Spoons* took a typical sitcom premise and turned it upside down. Preteen Ricky Stratton was a buttoned-up, Richie Rich–type boy sent to live with his father, a millionaire who loved to play with toys—literally. The charming series focused on a rebonding of father and son while each tries to make the other more like himself.

RICKY SCHRODER

(Born March 4, 1970)

Character: Ricky Stratton

Ricky made the transition from child star to adult star with concentrated effort. As the youngest award winner of the coveted Golden Globe, for best new male star for his role in *The Champ* when he was nine years old, as of 2015 he is still the youngest to have received a Golden Globe. After starring in a few minor films he got his big break with *Silver Spoons*. When the show was canceled and he struggled for new roles, he was advised to change his name to Rick to help in this endeavor. It seemed to work, as he began starring in more mature roles and stretching his acting abilities.

In 1992 he married Andrea Bernard, an interior designer and now TV fixture on Hallmark's *Home and Family*, and they have four children, two of whom have followed in their father's footsteps and appeared in TV and film. Rick obviously did not see any harm in his childhood career; in fact, he changed his name back to Ricky. He added directing to his creative palette in 2004 with the film *Black Cloud*. He owns the Ricky Schroder Production Company and produced the Hallmark movie *Our Wild Hearts* that he wrote, directed, and starred in with his daughter, Cambrie. His own good heart has led him to help build water wells in Guatemala via the Wells of Hope organization and to support the Cadet Youth Academy program, which helps steer wayward youth to a successful path. A strong sense of self emerged from his early career, and a firm family unit continues to add to his success.

ALFONSO RIBEIRO

(Born September 21, 1971)
Character: Alfonso Spears

After his debut in a PBS show, *Oye Ollie*, Alfonso displayed one of his many talents by grabbing the starring role on Broadway in *The Tap Dance Kid*. Thereafter,

Michael Jackson selected him for one of the dancers in a Pepsi commercial, and then Alfonso nabbed the part of Ricky's best friend in *Silver Spoons*. He attended Cal State–Los Angeles and went on to garner the role of Carlton in the long-running *The Fresh Prince of Bel Air* series, where he developed signature dance moves that came to be known as . . . the Carlton. He used his stardom to good effect as the winner of *Celebrity Duets*, topping Lucy Lawless, and on other competition shows before he exercised his special talent and rhythm to be crowned winner in the nineteenth season of *Dancing with the Stars* over Sadie Robertson and her partner. He has been married twice and has one child. After gaining experience as host of several TV shows, in 2015 Alfonso was knighted as the replacement for Tom Bergeron as host of *America's Funniest Home Videos*. This ex–child star is still dancing, happily, all the way to the bank.

Kate & Allie

6 Seasons: 122 episodes

Network: CBS; Color

Debut: March 19, 1984 / Finale: May 22, 1989

Reminiscent of the original situation on *The Lucy Show*, *Kate & Allie* blends the families of two divorced single moms who pool their resources into one house to make ends meet. It was one of the highest-rated and most critically acclaimed sitcoms of the 1980s.

ARI MEYERS

(Born April 6, 1969)

Character: Emma Jane McArdle

Ari, an admitted workaholic, started her efforts early as Al Pacino's stepdaughter in the film *Author! Author!* While working on *Kate & Allie*, she combined her acting chores with a full load of academics. She then left the show in the sixth season so, with her savings, she could go to Yale. Ari graduated with honors and a double degree in philosophy and theatre. She continued acting in TV-movies and films and then began recording voice-overs and narrating audio books. She wrote a book of her own, *The Triumphant Beautiful Egg*, a children's story that was recorded by Jeremy Irons and included in an anthology. She now focuses on her charitable organization, My Purpose Party, whose mission is to help people unlock their own innate creativity by doing the things they love to do and being of service to the world—a hefty goal but already being implemented by the slight, five-foot-one dynamo.

FRED KOEHLER

(Born June 16, 1975)
Character: Chip Lowell

Debuting as the oldest child in the film *Mr. Mom,* Fred continued his family portrayals by accepting the role of Chip in *Kate & Allie* for five seasons. When the show ended, the carrot-topped youth headed to Los Angeles and graduated from Beverly Hills High School. He claims this transition was a bit of a culture shock from his Queens, New York, beginnings. He decided to go to Carnegie Mellon College and graduated with a degree in theatre arts. After university he acted in plays, films, and TV, having successfully changed his cute image to portray roles such as neo-Nazis and characters with depth. In battling fast-life temptations, he opted for education and a degree of sanity. To him, "you have to make choices." It seems his choices so far have been excellent and rational ones.

ALLISON SMITH

(Born December 9, 1969)
Character: Jennie Lowell

Another redhead, Allison began her career on Broadway in *Evita* and then portrayed the title role in *Annie* for three years, beginning at the age of ten. She claims to have loved the experience and discovered many techniques for swaying an audience. She then was cast in the Emmy-winning *Kate & Allie*, shot in New York, a boon to Allison, who still had brothers and sisters at her home in the city. She attended NYU while she was involved with the series. Allison continued working after the show; she was especially noteworthy in her recurring part as Mallory O'Brien in *West Wing* for seven seasons. She is married to an attorney and they have two daughters who keep her busy. Allison is still singing, writing, and acting. She says of her child star experiences: "The positives of child acting are getting the jobs and having the experiences and doing the work. The negatives are auditioning and not getting the work and then involving rejection into your existence that wouldn't normally be there." Well said, Allison.

The Cosby Show

8 Seasons: 202 episodes

Network: NBC; Color

Debut: September 20, 1984 / Finale: April 30, 1992

The Cosby Show joins the ranks of *I Love Lucy* and *All in the Family* as a game-changing series. By the fall of 1984, the sitcom format was seen as on life-support at best. Most of the hits from the 1970s had ended or were ending their long runs, and the newer shows were lacking . . . something. That something turned out to be *The Cosby Show*. Cliff and Claire Huxtable are a successful doctor-and-lawyer couple with five children in a chaotic household in New York City. Dr. Cosby proclaimed the show and those that followed it to be part of a new Golden Age of comedy that launched in the '80s and lasted through much of the '90s. He said its success was due to a simple formula: Find humor in everyday situations, and rely on and honor the wisdom of one's elders rather than making wisecracking kids the center of a family sitcom. *Cosby* launched a generation of new series with wise parents in control of their kids in spite of financial or other circumstances, and television became fun again.

The cast of *The Cosby Show*, Season 1. Shown from left: Malcolm-Jamal Warner, Keshia Knight Pulliam, Bill Cosby, Phylicia Rashad, Lisa Bonet; front: Tempestt Bledsoe, c. 1984–85.
NBC/Photofest

MALCOLM-JAMAL WARNER

(Born August 18, 1970)

Character: Theodore "Theo" Huxtable

Love of performing even as a small child has kept Malcolm busy throughout his career. After a couple of small parts, he landed the role of Theo and during filming even found time to perform on other shows, including the *Cosby* spin-off, *A Different World,* and *The Fresh Prince of Bel Air*. Other series work was attained by Malcolm in *Here and Now, The Magic School Bus,* and *Malcolm and Eddie*. He kept working with recurring roles on *Jeremiah, Listen Up, Major Crimes,* and *Sons of Anarchy*. He produced, directed, and starred in the BET series *Reed Between the Lines*. Besides his acting Malcolm has directed music videos and performed with the jazz funk band Miles Long. He won a Grammy for his collaboration with The Robert Glasper Experience and Lalah Hathaway on the song "Jesus Children." Malcolm has been a very busy ex–child star.

LISA BONET

(Born November 16, 1967)
Character: Denise Huxtable

Of Louisiana Creole descent, Lisa was cast in *The Cosby Show* after appearing in commercials in Los Angeles. When she tried to break her image in the wholesome show by starring in a skin flick called *Angel* in 1987, she was released from *Cosby* and spun over to *A Different World*. When she stopped showing up on time and started exhibiting other unprofessional behavior, she was fired from that show. She ultimately returned to *Cosby* for two more seasons beginning in the fall of 1989 before leaving for good at the end of the seventh season. Lisa married soon-to-become-famous rocker Lenny Kravitz, and they had a child, Zoe. When this relationship ended, she married *Game of Thrones* actor Jason Momoa, and they have one child. She tagged two more series—*Life on M*ars in 2008 and *The Red Road* in 2014. She spends much of her time as an activist and as a creator: "I'm writing a film. With our access to these powerful media we're going to take over because it's really disgusting what is put out here to be consumed." This ex–child star who claimed to be shy has found her voice.

TEMPESTT BLEDSOE

(Born August 1, 1973)
Character: Vanessa Huxtable

Tempestt emerged from her experience on *The Cosby Show* with a good sense of self, she says, which allowed her to graduate from college—NYU—and be selective of the roles she chose to play. She has stated that she was uncommonly close to Mr. Cosby. Tempestt appeared on many reality shows after the series, including her own talk show, *The Tempestt Bledsoe Show,* as well as *Clean House* on the Style Network, *Celebrity Fit,* and *Househusbands of Hollywood.* In 2012 she agreed to star in the NBC series *Guys with Kids* as the character of Marney. Pretty good for a kid who started out hawking Frosted Flakes.

KESHIA KNIGHT PULLIAM

(Born April 9, 1979)
Character: Rudy Huxtable

The youngest Huxtable, Keshia had already enjoyed a nice career in showbiz in commercials and TV before she plucked the plum role of Rudy at the age of six. After the show, she went to Foxcroft School and graduated from Spelman College with a degree in sociology in 2001. Since then, her show business appearances have included *The Fear Factor, The Weakest Link,* and the 2015 season of *The Apprentice*. She has done some film but seems to relish the small screen, with a recurring part in Tyler Perry's *House of Payne* as Miranda Lucas Payne. Keshia had a great experience on *The Cosby Show* and has defended her former "father" from the accusations against him.

Mr. Belvedere

6 Seasons: 117 episodes

Network: ABC; Color

Debut: March 15, 1985 / Finale: July 8, 1990

The Owens household was an out-of-control three-ring circus where the inmates (the kids) were in charge of the asylum (the household). Then Mr. Belvedere arrived. Although he was not initially welcomed with open arms, the parents quickly discovered that Mr. Belvedere possessed the parenting skills and authority they were sorely lacking. The chemistry of this cast keeps this show fresh decades later.

ROB STONE

(Born September 26, 1962)
Character: Kevin Owens

Although Rob was twenty-three when he accepted the part of Kevin Owens, he was to play a teen—typical of Hollywood casting. He had stage experience, had attended USC in theatre arts, and had played some roles in series like *Silver Spoons* and *The Facts of Life,* so he was prepared for the sitcom world. The Texas native decided to follow a different path than acting but stay in the business, so he founded a production company to produce documentaries. His first project starred his friend from *Mr. Belvedere,* Christopher Hewett. Finding this work satisfying, he continues in the field. Rob has produced a two-hour documentary on the Blue Angels and is still creating movies and TV series, notably *Shank!* in Los Angeles, where he lives with his wife, Melissa Chan Stone.

TRACY WELLS

(Born March 13, 1971)
Character: Heather Owens

A native of Southern California, Tracy had two TV credits before she was given the part of Heather. Appearing in 118 episodes of the series seemed to have satisfied her Hollywood itch, although she did make three more TV appearances before she retired. She still lives in California, but is married and has two children. As Tracy Tofte, she enjoys her role as successful real estate agent, and she presents houses with aplomb and appeal.

BRICE BECKHAM

(Born February 11, 1976)
Character: Wesley T. Owens

As the youngest of the Owens clan, Wesley seemed to give Mr. Belvedere the most trouble, and he still seems to be stirring the cauldron with jibes at fellow actors, like Kirk Cameron for comments that went against Brice's beliefs. When the series was no longer, Brice stayed away from the Hollywood scene until he returned as a triple threat, writing, directing, and producing VH1's short-lived *I Hate My 30's*. He continued on this path and produced four more TV series until he wrote and produced twelve episodes of *Crash Pad*. He is painting, acting in theatre, playing in a band, and continuing to develop projects where he can be in control.

Small Wonder

4 Seasons: 96 episodes

Network: Syndicated; Color

Debut: September 7, 1985 / Finale: May 20, 1989

Small Wonder holds the crown for being one of the worst sitcoms ever, but it's also, conversely, a delightful one because of the performance of child star lead Tiffany Brissette. Sophomoric humor, bad jokes, and horrendous puns made the show itself the butt of jokes, but Brissette's performance as Vicki the Robot brilliantly brought life to an otherwise dreadful concept: a human-looking, human-acting robot that learned by living among other children. Despite her monotone voice (reminiscent of the *Lost in Space* robot), her neighbors and schoolmates never caught on that she was not a real girl but only a machine.

The cast of *Small Wonder*. Emily Schulman, Dick Christie, Jerry Supiran, Marla Pennington, Tiffany Brissette.

20th Century Fox/Photofest

TIFFANY BRISSETTE

(Born December 26, 1974)

Character: Victoria Ann Smith-Lawson/Vicki the Robot

Tiffany's adorable voice landed her roles in animated shows and commercials when she was just a babe of two. Soaring with the *Wonder* role of the "Voice Input Child Identicant," or "V.I.C.I.," her robot persona became more humanized as the series progressed, and her frilly red dress was exchanged for more modern wear. When the series ended, Tiffany acted in a few more roles but was essentially done with Hollywood. She graduated from Westmont College in Santa Barbara with a degree in psychology—probably to try to figure out the differences between robots and real servants—and was a nanny for a year in Boulder, Colorado. She now lives there, has studied nursing, and cares for real live human beings.

JERRY SUPIRAN

(Born March 21, 1973)

Character: Jamie Lawson

Vicki's human brother in the series discovered some inhumanity in his later life. When the show was finished, he also found his bank account finished, that is, depleted. He accused managers of stealing from him, and strippers and other lady friends of taking advantage of his good nature. He worked odd jobs and then as a waiter in Henderson, Nevada, until he was laid off in 2010. He then lived in central

California, homeless and in search of something more substantial than transitory robotic females. Jerry's conditions are still sad, but he has been working toward restoring order and has recently reached out to the ex–child star network to help him get a new agent and a new life.

EMILY SCHULMAN

(Born August 17, 1977)
Character: Harriet Brindle

Feisty, redheaded Emily was a natural for commercials, in which she started appearing at the tender age of two. After romping through *Small Wonder* she garnered a part in the movie *Troop Beverly Hills* and then retired from acting; her last show was on the TV series *Christy*. She remained in the city of bright lights and became the head of the commercial department for ACME Talent & Literary. She married Derek Webster in 2002, and they now have four children. Perhaps to escape the Hollywood life, the family moved to Connecticut, where Emily is happily teaching acting to fledgling child stars.

Growing Pains

7 Seasons: 166 episodes
Network: ABC; Color
Debut: September 24, 1985 / Finale: April 25, 1992

The Seaver family of *Growing Pains* was modeled after the successful new sitcom format of *The Cosby Show*: smart kids and smarter parents in an upscale community. This is the show that launched Kirk Cameron as a teen superstar and, later on, introduced the world to an actor named Leonardo DiCaprio.

KIRK CAMERON

(Born October 12, 1970)
Character: Mike Seaver

Evangelical Christian Kirk began his career in commercials at the suggestion of his friend, actor Adam Rich. The nine-year-old segued to TV parts and netted a series,

A scene from *Growing Pains*. Shown from left: Tracey Gold, Jeremy Miller, Alan Thicke, Joanna Kerns, Kirk Cameron. *ABC/Photofest*

Two Marriages, which was quickly canceled. His break came when he garnered the role on *Growing Pains* at thirteen; he grew up on the show and became a teen idol. This fame led Kirk to say, "The Hollywood lifestyle was just overwhelming. A party here, an interview there, magazine and modeling shoots daily, your face everywhere and girls throwing themselves at you. As great as I felt at the time, I still felt something missing and I needed to change." What he felt was missing was God, and he became a born-again Christian at seventeen.

When the show ended Kirk skewed his life to serving God and founded a ministry with Ray Comfort called The Way of the Master, which also features a website, *Living Waters,* and a cable TV show that he cohosts. Kirk also acts in faith-based films such as the blockbuster *Fireproof* and *Saving Christmas.* He and his wife, Chelsea Noble, whom he met on the set of *Growing,* married in 1991 and have six children, four of whom are adopted. The Camerons established The Firefly Foundation, which provides a camp for terminally ill children in Georgia. In 2008 Kirk wrote the book *Still Growing: An Autobiography* on how family and faith provided him the ballast to smile and find an important path where he can continue to grow and achieve. Kirk managed to avoid the child star stereotype and is lighting a path for others.

TRACEY GOLD

(Born May 16, 1969)

Character: Carol Seaver

Having a father as a successful talent agent is always a career boost, and Tracey received hers at just five years of age. From commercials she segued to starring in her first show, the TV-movie *Roots,* essaying the part of Sandy Duncan's character as a child. Following this appearance and two short-lived series, *Shirley* with Shirley Jones and *Goodnight, Beantown* with Bill Bixby, she was catapulted to teen fame—and anorexia—in 1984 on *Growing Pains*. When Tracey was reduced to eighty pounds and refused to eat, the producers suspended her from the show. She did return for the last two episodes of the series in 1992. After recovering from her eating disorder, she became a TV-movie queen, starring in a raft of made-for-television movies. Joanna Kerns, her *Growing Pains* mother, introduced Tracey to actor Rob Marshall. They married in 1994 and have four children.

In September of 2004, Tracey was arrested for drunk driving: She was driving her SUV with her three sons and her husband as passengers when she lost control and crashed down an embankment. Her youngest son at the time, Sage, suffered a broken clavicle and face lacerations. She was charged with a felony DUI. She continues her career in film, TV, and reality programming. In 2012 she produced and hosted the series *Starving Secrets* for Lifetime. Swallowing a large dose of reality from her exploits and from writing her autobiography, *Room to Grow: An Appetite for Life*, she strives for happiness, balance, and a satisfying family life. However, it ain't easy being a star.

JEREMY MILLER

(Born October 21, 1976)

Character: Ben Seaver

The youngest addition to the Seaver family, Jeremy first started appearing in commercials and then appeared on *Punky Brewster* before he landed the part of Ben. *Growing Pains*—the series and two reunion films—was about it for his acting career, although he did perform in a role for *Milk and Fashion,* a Chinese fusion movie. His tale of alcohol abuse is well documented: When the series was done, so was Jeremy. Not finding work and in an awkward stage—it's tough growing up in front of millions of TV fans sporting a mullet and acne—he started drinking heavily and was in a dark place for fifteen years before he joined the Fresh Start Private Recovery program. During that time he married his wife and took in her three sons. Although he has worked at odd jobs, his passion is cooking, and he has tried to break into the culinary arts. He still wants to dabble in acting, however. He's had an appetizer, full course, and now past his difficult teen transition stage, he is looking for his just "desserts." He's skipping the wine with dinner, though.

ASHLEY JOHNSON

(Born August 9, 1983)
Character: Chrissy Seaver

Ashley showed up on *Growing Pains* in the last two seasons, playing a six-year-old. Evidently her character, Chrissy, had some odd genes, as the season before she was just a baby (played by twins Kirsten and Kelsey Dohring). When the show ended, she continued working as a regular in five more TV series, albeit short-lived, before her nasal voice found work in such animated shows as *Jumanji* and *Recess* and then more recent cartoon series such as *Pound Puppies* and *Teen Titans*. Ashley, from her child star days, happily remained a child at heart and became the TV cartoon series kid. She also runs the company Infinity Pictures with her friend and production assistant Mila Shah, and so far she doesn't seem to be suffering any of the angst of an ex–child star.

LEONARDO DiCAPRIO

(Born November 11, 1974)
Character: Luke Brower

Talk about a successful ex–child star! Leo began his career acting in commercials and educational films. Retaining a talent agent, who suggested that he change his name to Lenny Williams, Leonardo took the idea into consideration and then decided to keep his own name. His talent was soon observed in a couple of guest spots on episodics by the producers of *Growing Pains*. To improve falling ratings and find another babe-catcher to supplant the waning popularity of Jeremy, the handsome Leonardo was discovered and cast in the last season of *Pains*. Even this megastar-to-be couldn't bolster the ratings, and the show was canceled. The once-popular *Pains* sitcom, although on a downward spiral when Leo joined them in 1991, gave the budding actor prominence and presence enough to secure the part of a homeless troubled youth in *What's Eating Gilbert Grape* and an Academy Award nomination for best supporting actor in the film. His career took a giant leap forward after this, even though he appeared in some low-budget horror flicks. His handsome looks and excellent talent quickly moved him up the theatrical ladder; he began starring in megapics and is still shining in excellent movies, even though he has yet to win the coveted Oscar—but he was nominated for his role in *The Revenant* and it looks very promising. . . . Here's an ex–child star with an exciting career and a success-filled life. It is possible.

Valerie/Valerie's Family/ Valerie's Family: The Hogans/ The Hogan Family

6 Seasons: 110 episodes

Network: NBC; Color

Debut: March 1, 1986 / Finale: July 20, 1991

Originally created as a star vehicle called *Valerie* for lead Valerie Harper of *Rhoda* fame, this show is more remembered for what to do with a show named for a star who refuses to report to work. While the sweet domestic sitcom most notably launched the career of teenage Jason Bateman, Valerie Harper turned sour when her salary demands were denied before Season 3 began filming, and she refused to show up for work. The solution? Change the name to *Valerie's Family,* say that Valerie died in a car accident during the summer hiatus (on the show, not in real life), and bring in Aunt Sandy (Sandy Duncan) to help raise the motherless boys. Then change the name again to *Valerie's Family: The Hogans*. Then change the name again to *The Hogan Family*. In any case, Harper's character would have been immediately forgotten if only her name hadn't remained in the title for so long.

The cast of *Valerie*. Shown clockwise from top left: Josh Taylor, Jason Bateman, Jeremy Licht, Luis Daniel Ponce; center: Valerie Harper.

NBC/Photofest

JASON BATEMAN

(Born January 14, 1969)

Character: David Hogan

The oldest of the sons on *The Hogan Family*, Jason, brother of Justine of *Family Ties* fame, had a great deal of experience before joining the show. Recurring roles on *Little House on the Prairie*, *Silver Spoons*, and *It's Your Move* had honed his skills and acceptance as a reliable child actor and then teen star. *The Hogan Family* was the show that inaugurated Jason's entrance into directing, and he started that process when he was merely eighteen. Jason is quoted as saying, "This is a tough town to live in if you're not relevant. I'm not making my decisions based on the fear of that. But there's a reason people have a long career and it's because they're doing respectful work. I really want to be in that group." See references to Jason "now" in his bio under *Little House on the Prairie*.

JEREMY LICHT

(Born January 4, 1971)

Character: Mark Hogan

Jeremy played the responsible fraternal twin to his brother Willie in *Valerie*. As a child, Jeremy had appeared in numerous TV-movies and films since the age of five. After the series, he acted in a couple of episodics and was then off to college to pursue other areas of show business—primarily the business part. The responsible nature of his character on *Valerie* shone through when he was accepted at USC and studied finance. He went on to intern with Merrill Lynch and then opened his own company, JL Capital Management. He seems to be handling his own capital wisely. Jeremy married Carol-Ann Plante, the teen star of *Harry and the Hendersons,* but the couple divorced in 2001. He then married Kimberly Wallis in 2007, and they have two children, Casey and Jordan. Jeremy says he is still open to entertaining offers—once an actor . . .

LUIS DANIEL PONCE

(Born September 4, 1972)
Character: Willie Hogan

Danny Ponce, as he was billed on the show, had many guest spots on TV series and even a ten-episode run on *Knots Landing* before *Valerie*. Playing the freewheeling twelve-year-old Willie appealed to Danny but not enough to keep him deeply in show business. After the series he continued to work in episodics, and he accepts a few jobs now and then. But he is most comfortable living a private life with his wife, the former Rachel Swan, whom he married in 2006, and their two children.

Starman

1 Season: 22 hour-long episodes

Network: ABC; Color

Debut: September 19, 1986 / Finale: May 2, 1987

This series is a segue from the film of the same name. In this outing, fifteen years after the events of the movie, an alien returns to Earth to meet and guide his teenage son, Scott Hayden Jr., while eluding the US government. Each week father and son move from place to place, helping local residents and avoiding detection by the military.

CHRISTOPHER DANIEL BARNES

(Born November 7, 1972)

Character: Scott Hayden Jr.

Christopher is probably known more for his voice career than for his on-camera acting, but he has gained fame for both. Moving from Portland, Maine, to New

York when he was eight years old, he started his career by acting in commercials and on the soap opera *As the World Turns* for two years. When the family again moved, this time to the West Coast, Christopher was cast as the half-alien/half-human son to Robert Hays in *Starman*. When that show was canceled, he segued to *Day by Day*, but it also only lasted one season. He gained most recognition for his voice portrayal of *Spider-Man* in the animated TV series of the same name that originally ran for four seasons. He also voiced Peter Parker in video games and the same character in the animated TV series *Ultimate Spider-Man*. Christopher channeled Greg Brady and appeared in two of the Brady franchise films. No academic slouch, he attained both a bachelor's and master's degree and wrote the book *The Warrior*. He is married to Rebecca Guyadeen and says about acting, "You can't judge an actor by the character he plays. An actor is a chameleon, his ability is bound by his imagination; his imagination is boundless." With this philosophy, one can see how he can leap from Spider-Man to Greg Brady so easily . . . and so well.

ALF

4 Seasons: 99 episodes
Network: NBC; Color
Debut: September 22, 1986 / Finale: March 24, 1990

ALF, or *A*lien *L*ife *F*orm, was a funny mid-'80s domestic comedy about a family with a special problem: a visitor with a Brooklyn accent who overstays his welcome and has an appetite for cats. But this visitor can't go home—he is an extraterrestrial who crashed on the family's house, and now they feel obligated to care for him. ALF himself was more reminiscent of a muppet, but the chemistry of the cast made this star shine.

ANDREA ELSON

(Born March 6, 1969)
Character: Lynn Tanner

Typical of ex–child stars, Andrea started appearing in print ads and commercials before she was hired to do on-screen work. Her debut was in the 1983 series *Whiz Kids,* in which she played a teenage detective. Recognition from this role led to her casting as Lynn in *ALF* as well as romance: She married Scott Hopper, who was a PA (production assistant) on the show. When the Alien Task Force captured ALF and the show was canceled, Andrea did a few sitcom episodics and then decided the acting realm was no longer her domain. She is now enjoying her own family "sitcom" in Los Angeles with her husband and daughter and without any extraterrestrial beings to disturb her happiness.

BENJI GREGORY

(Born May 26, 1978)
Character: Brian Tanner

Benji came from a true acting family affair: His father, uncles, and sister were all actors; his grandmother was a theatrical agent. Of course, Benji would be led to follow in tradition. However, the theatrical appeal only lasted a short while. He stated that he didn't like acting and, after his stint on *ALF*, he went into voice-over but said, "I was in a lot of stupid cartoons . . . Voice-overs are easy, and I wasn't actively trying to act anymore." He began studying at the Academy of Art in San Francisco, but found the military more to his liking and joined the navy in 2004, where he served as an aerographer's mate. Now, as Ben Hertzberg, he and his wife, Sarah, live in Arizona. Ship ahoy.

Married . . . with Children

11 Seasons: 259 episodes

Network: Fox; Color

Debut: April 5, 1987 / Finale: June 9, 1997

One of the fledgling Fox network's first programs was also one of its longest-running—the irreverent *Married . . . with Children*. This domestic comedy took the prevailing *Cosby*-esque sitcom format dominating the medium by 1987 and turned it on its ear: Not only were the kids smarter than the parents, but the parents didn't really care—about each other, about the kids, or about the neighbors. And despite the show's mean-spirited humor, the cast delivered it in such a lighthearted way that they made mean humor fun.

CHRISTINA APPLEGATE

(Born November 25, 1971)
Character: Kelly Bundy

Playing the character of a stereotypical dumb blonde didn't seem to faze Christina, as she played many different roles as a child before she was cast in *Married . . . with Children.* Her mother was an actress and would take Christina with her to auditions, where Christina absorbed a good sense of the business. With a single mother and both of them working to making make ends meet, Christina is a good example of how child actors sometimes contribute to the household income. There was an incredible bond established between her and her mother. When the series ended, Christina continued to work steadily in the business—it was in her blood—and she was honored for her work onstage and in movies. She has overcome breast cancer and child actor syndrome to come to a spiritual place where she enjoys her husband and child and looks forward to each new day.

DAVID FAUSTINO

(Born March 3, 1974)
Character: Bud Bundy

David Faustino joined the dysfunctional Bundy family at thirteen after appearing in many TV shows and on the big screen. He has always embraced his theatrical life and found that the series incorporated many of the same trials and challenges he was experiencing as he spent eleven years growing up on the show. When the series ended, he continued his theatrical pursuits, adding writer, rapper, and radio host to his briefcase of talents. David and his first wife, Andrea, were married from 2004 to 2007. David now has a daughter, born in 2015, with girlfriend Lindsay Bronson.

He has been arrested for marijuana possession, but now that he is a father, he watches his intake. It was rumored that there was to be a spin-off of *Married . . . with Children* with David in a starring role. Now that David has a child of his own, why not?

My Two Dads

3 Seasons: 60 episodes

Network: NBC; Color

Debut: September 20, 1987 / Finale: April 30, 1990

When twelve-year-old Nicole's mom dies, she has to go live with her dad. Problem is, no one knows who her father is—it could be one of two fellows, and Mom never took the initiative to find out which one the baby daddy was. So for now Nicole has two dads, and since they both want to raise her, they set up a household together and bring in the motherless girl.

STACI KEANAN

(Born June 6, 1975)

Character: Nicole Bradford

Stacy maintained high scholastics interspersed with her modeling and theatre acting duties as a young girl on the East Coast. Those skills and knowledge held her in good stead when she semiretired from her screen acting career and became a lawyer. After her starring stint on *My Two Dads* she bagged another series, *Step by Step,* in 1991 with Patrick Duffy, Suzanne Somers, and Christine Lakin (among other 'tweens and teens). After a ten-year hiatus from the business, during which she attended and graduated from UCLA, she reunited with Patrick and Christine in the film *You Again* in 2010. She also made twenty-first-century appearances in *Death and Creation* and *Holyman Undercover.* Stacey (she changed the spelling supposedly to convey more maturity) still takes on screen roles but is now a wife, and mother of two, and she primarily practices the true art of acting as an attorney in Los Angeles.

Full House

8 Seasons: 192 episodes

Network: ABC; Color

Debut: September 22, 1987 / Finale: May 23, 1995

This long-running Friday-night staple in ABC's must-see teen programming is still a favorite among millennials. When a man is suddenly widowed and forced to raise three small girls alone, his best friend and his brother-in-law move in to give him a hand. Early humor focused on watching men learn to do jobs traditionally handled in the household by the mom. As the years passed, the family grew as one of the men married and added twin boys to the household. Full house indeed!

The cast of *Full House*. Shown clockwise from lower left: Jodie Sweetin, Candace Cameron, Scott Weinger, Mary-Kate/Ashley Olsen, Andrea Barber, Dave Coulier, Bob Saget, Lori Loughlin, John Stamos, 1993.

ABC/Photofest

CANDACE CAMERON

(Born April 6, 1976)

Character: D. J. Tanner

As Kirk's younger sister, Candace was used to a houseful of child actors. After her debut in commercials at the age of five, she remained on *Full House* for all eight seasons. After the series, she took a hiatus and married hockey star Valeri Bure; they have three children—another full house. She reentered the acting market and garnered a role on the TV series *Make It or Break It* and in several TV-movies for the Hallmark Channel. As Candace Cameron Bure, she authored two *New York Times* bestsellers *Reshaping It All: Motivation for Physical and Spiritual Fitness* and *Balancing It All: My Story of Juggling Priorities and Purpose.* She came in third in Season 18 of *Dancing with the Stars,* which inspired her third book, *Dancing through Life: Steps of Courage and Conviction.* Sharing the faith of her brother and her husband, Candace travels to give inspirational speeches to others and participate in many charities She has stated that she will join the other past stars of *Full House* on a new series, *Fuller House,* on Netflix, and that she enjoyed her years on *Full House* and as a child star. She must have, because she's populated her house with adorable children and her internal "house" with love and inspiration.

JODIE SWEETIN

(Born January 18, 1982)

Character: Stephanie Tanner

Jodie began her career at four years old doing commercials that continued until she landed the part of the middle child in *Full House.* Middling attention may have been the reason she got hooked on methamphetamines, but she fully describes her experiences with cocaine, alcohol, and meth in her memoir, *UnSweetined*. She tells how she was living a double life, presenting a happy, wholesome persona while secretly taking drugs to hide the anguish of doubts and low self-esteem. Becoming a mother with her first child, by Cody Herpin, helped her on the road to recovery, she has said, although she suffers scars from her former addictions. She married her third husband, musician Morty Cole, in 2012 and had her second child with him. Jodie filed for legal separation in 2014. She still claims acting as her profession, although she tried a hosting stint for *Pants Off Dance Off* competitions. A TV sequel to the original *Full House* has been announced with Jodie taking part. This involvement might quell the rumors of her desire to become a teacher, even though she graduated from Chapman College. This is one ex–child star who had to fight to conquer the wrong choices she made as a teenager, but she claims she has been clean and sober since 2008. Good for her.

MARY-KATE OLSEN
ASHLEY OLSEN

(Twins born on June 13, 1986)

Character: Michelle Tanner

The Mary-Kate and Ashley franchise is known to millions who have bought wares from their design lines and DVDs of their string of TV-movies. This is an ex–child star success story . . . or is it? Beginning their career as babies, Mary-Kate and Ashley grew up on the set of *Full House* while forward-looking and experienced managers took over and used their celebrity on the show to lead them to fortune. Rumored use of sex, drugs, and rock and roll especially came into play when Ashley was reported to have been the last person to see Heath Ledger alive. His autopsy revealed that he had overdosed on prescription drugs. The twins continue on their gilded path but primarily oversee their vast fortune by running their fashion-design labels. They received the Women's Designer of the Year Award from the Council of Fashion Designers of America in 2014. Sometimes it can be very lucrative and exciting to enter show business virtually at birth. Ashley and Mary-Kate are often referred to as ex–baby stars.

Star Trek: The Next Generation

7 Seasons: 176 episodes

Network: Syndicated; Color

Debut: September 28, 1987 / Finale: May 23, 1994

The original *Star Trek* ran for three seasons on NBC in the late '60s. While ratings at the time could not justify a fourth season, the series became a cult classic in reruns and a mega money machine as the basis for movies, beginning with *Star Trek: The Motion Picture* in 1979. Creator Gene Roddenberry brought his show back with a new cast and new ship in this syndicated series that was a surprise hit and the beginning of a string of *Star Trek* series that stretched for years into the twenty-first century.

WIL WHEATON

(Born July 29, 1972)

Character: Wesley Crusher

Wil has been quoted as saying, "When you say a 'former child star,' you may as well say 'failed child star.'" That really doesn't make sense, but he has said he doesn't make sense to himself. Gaining a starring part in the film *Stand by Me* as a child, he continued his youthful acting pursuits until he gained fandom in the *Star Trek* series. An admitted geek, he went to Kansas to rid himself of some anger issues and worked as a techie, not a trekkie. Returning to California he took acting lessons for five years and then reentered the entertainment industry. He has had roles in TV, films, voice-over, and audio narration. Wil has assembled some of his blog ramblings and published both print and audio versions of *Dancing Barefoot* and *Just a Geek*. He calls his wife, Anne, "the most awesome person in the universe," and they have two children. He appears at occasional *Star Trek* conventions and continues his personal Wil Wheaton ex–child star projects.

The Wonder Years

6 Seasons: 115 episodes
Network: ABC; Color
Debut: January 31, 1988 / Finale: May 12, 1993

The title of this series is derived from a brand of bread that was popular with kids in the 1960s: Wonder Bread. Its white plastic wrap had colorful balloons on it, and it was pitched by Captain Kangaroo. *The Wonder Years* echoes back to the teen years of the present-day narrator, which were in the late 1960s and early 1970s. Fred Savage became an American favorite on this charming single-camera comedy that did not rely on a live audience or laugh track to cue the viewer to laugh. For baby boomers, this show was a treasure trove of memories of their own years of wonder.

A scene from *The Wonder Years*. Josh Saviano, Fred Savage, Danica McKellar.
ABC/Photofest

FRED SAVAGE

(Born July 9, 1976)

Character: Kevin Arnold

Award-winning actor Fred Savage is an example of how ex–child stars can transition from a youth to an adult who lives a successful life. He has said, "It is unfortunate that the poor judgment shown by a small group of young actors has tarnished the reputation of every child who has ever appeared before a camera." Wise words. I believe Freddy was able to establish his longevity in the business through smart choices and an excellent education. After his debut in the movie (*The Boy Who Could Fly*) and TV series (*Morningstar/Eveningstar*), Fred worked steadily for three years in TV roles until he was cast in the starring role of Kevin in *The Wonder Years*. After the show, he continued taking on various acting parts, attended and graduated from Stanford University with a degree in English, and started a second career behind the camera as a prolific director and producer. He married his childhood sweetheart in 2004, and they have three children. In 2015 he was offered the part in the new series *The Grinder,* costarring with Rob Lowe, where Fred plays a lawyer in a small town and Rob plays his celebrity brother whose role as a lawyer in a TV series has just ended. Second careers can go hand in hand with the vast experience garnered by child actors if their choices are correct and support is strong.

OLIVIA D'ABO

(Born January 22, 1969)
Character: Karen Arnold

Born into an acting family in London, beautiful Olivia continued the tradition with her early appearances in the movies *Conan the Barbarian* and *Bolero*. She kept working in TV until she was chosen for the role of Kevin's hippie sister for four seasons. Her longevity in the acting business was secured after the series by stints in voice-over, theatrical presentations, and her songwriting and musical performances. The triple-threat actor proves how expanding one's presence in the entertainment world by taking on different roles in different fields can lead to success and belie the ex–child star stereotype. Olivia, once engaged to Julian Lennon, married songwriter Patrick Leonard in 2001. The couple had one son, Oliver, but they divorced in 2012. Olivia continues her sterling career by shining in TV, movies, animation, and music.

JASON HERVEY

(Born April 6, 1972)
Character: Wayne Arnold

Another child star to leverage his long experience in the entertainment industry is Jason Hervey. The 250 commercials to his credit as a child helped him land excellent roles in television series before he was cast in his signature role as Wayne in *The Wonder Years*. After the show wrapped, he took the knowledge he gained on the show and segued to behind-the-camera duties. He learned to direct and produce, established relationships with production houses, and even worked for a time for a Fortune 500 company in marketing. He and his friend Eric Bischoff are the cofounders of Bischoff Hervey Entertainment (BHE TV); they create, license, and distribute content to broadcasters. Jason and his wife, Shannon, have two children and, through his hard work and perseverance, two homes, one in Los Angeles and one in Arizona. from which to shuttle his adult ideas and projects.

JOSH SAVIANO

(Born March 31, 1976)
Character: Paul Joshua Pfeiffer

Ex–child stars who have quit the business seem to be drawn to the legal profession. And why not? They already have loads of experience being in front of people and putting on an act. Josh was no exception; he began his act when he was twelve, doing commercials and small parts on TV before he was deemed just right to play the part of a dorky friend on *The Wonder Years*. In the last season, his character wanted to go to law school. It seems Josh is a method actor! After graduating from Yale University and working as a paralegal, he did go to law school and passed the New York bar. He is now practicing his lines in court. Josh and his wife, who is also an attorney, have one daughter, Noa, who has not expressed any acting aspirations thus far.

DANICA McKELLAR

(Born January 3, 1975)

Character: Gwendolyn "Winnie" Cooper

Beginning as a dancer who trained at her mother's studio, Danica pirouetted into her breakthrough role as Winnie after a couple of jobs acting in commercials and on TV. She attained a significant post-series career in voice-over, but she is also known for recurring appearances on *The West Wing, NCIS,* and *Strong Medicine,* among others. She is a math whiz, having graduated summa cum laude from UCLA with a degree in that field. *Kiss My Math* and *Math Doesn't Suck* are just two of the *New York Times* best-selling books she has written. Danica had one child with husband Mike Verta before they divorced in 2013. Danica married Scott Svelosky in 2014. She continues to both work in the entertainment business and present erudite speeches on statistical mechanics. Danica figured out how to combine variables in entertainment, mathematics, and motherhood to add up to and create one successful life for an ex–child star.

Just the Ten of Us

3 Seasons: 47 episodes

Network: ABC; Color

Debut: April 26, 1988 / Finale: May 4, 1990

This *Growing Pains* spin-off followed the former gym teacher at the Seavers' high school after he was laid off and forced to relocate his family of eight children. In a financial bind, the father gets special permission for his teenage daughters to attend the all-boys academy at which he will now be working, to the chagrin of the school's administration.

HEATHER LANGENKAMP

(Born July 17, 1964)

Character: Marie Lubbock

As one of our older child actors, Heather first appeared in the movies *Nickel Mountain* and *The Outsiders* as an extra when she was a teen. As it turned out, her scenes were cut from those movies, but definitely not from her follow-up films in the *A Nightmare on Elm Street* franchise, where she was a teen scream queen. *Just the Ten of Us* came her way and she gladly accepted something a little less frightening than the horror dream films she had been making. Enamored of the prosthetic and specialized makeup worn in the horror movies, she and her second husband, David Leroy Anderson, whom she married in 1990, opened AFX Studio in Panorama City, California, which is a full-service special makeup effects shop. She graduated from Stanford University, has two children, and lives in Malibu. Her take on the movie and acting scene: "I like acting but it is just something that I do on the side; being rich and famous is not a priority for me." Although she completed two films in 2014 and 2015, Heather backs up her words by spending time with her family, at the PTA, and in a local beach cleanup effort.

JAMIE LUNER

(Born May 12, 1971)

Character: Cynthia "Cindy" Lubbock

Jamie has had a steady career in show business and is still going strong, beginning in commercials when she was only three years old. While attending Beverly Hills High School she was cast in *Growing Pains* and then the spin-off, *Just the Ten of Us,* as a regular. When the show was canceled, she decided her artistry emanated more from the kitchen, and so she went to culinary school to become a chef. Finding messy food cleanups not so much to her liking, she still dreams of having a restaurant someday. She reentered show business with appearances on episodics and then got her break as Peyton Richards on the TV series *Savannah*. She followed this as Lexi Sterling on *Melrose Place* and graduated to the TV series *The Profiler*. Starring in one-season series seemed to be following her around until she landed the role of Liza Colby in the soap *All My Children* until it was canceled in 2011. When she left that show she continued to act in TV-movies and episodics, primarily as the "sexy vixen." She says: "Fame definitely has its effects. A lot is relative. You gain so much with fame, and in the same respect you give up quite a bit—the most precious being my anonymity, which I didn't realize until it was gone."

BROOKE THEISS

(Born October 23, 1969)
Character: Wendy Lubbock

As the younger twin sister to Cindy, Wendy was another character spinning off from *Growing Pains* to find a home on *Just the Ten of Us*. On this series she joined the other Lubbock sisters in the show in a fictional singing group, The Lubbock Babes, but none of them pursued a musical career. Although diagnosed with dyslexia, Brooke found work in films, most notably *A Nightmare on Elm Street 4: The Dream Master* (other Lubbock sisters also appeared in the *Nightmare* franchise) and in three short-lived series: *Good and Evil, Home Free,* and *The Amanda Show*. Continuing to take small parts in TV shows and commercials, she married Canadian actor Bryan Genesse in 1994, who had appeared in an episode of *Just the Ten of Us*. Brooke bore two children, a son and daughter, and just the four of them have found comfort and joy.

JOANN WILLETTE

(Born October 12, 1963)
Character: Constance "Connie" Lubbock

As the fourth teenage Lubbock daughter, Connie was characterized as the "bohemian." JoAnn also appeared in the *A Nightmare on Elm Street* film series, *A Nightmare on Elm Street 2: Freddy's Revenge.* Evidently *Just the Ten of Us* taught the girls to deal with bad dreams—or not. After the series she appeared in guest spots on TV, but her résumé is rather thin. JoAnn has since gone on to write screenplays, perform at storytelling venues, and present one-woman shows following her own path. Her latest show, *Unfictional,* has gotten great reviews. She still continues to take on acting jobs, but as an ex–child star has found other ways to apply her talent and creativity.

MATT SHAKMAN

(Born August 8, 1975)
Character: Graham "J. R." Lubbock Jr.

Although Matt began his career at four years of age, his first TV screen appearance was on the *Facts of Life* at nine. He worked steadily as a child actor until he was cast as Matt in the *Just the Ten of Us* series. Then he left the business for a while and graduated from Yale with a dual major of theatre and history, where his interests turned to directing. He is now an award-winning director in both prime-time TV and theatre. Assignments for television included his first foray with *Once and Again* and *Still Life* to his 2015 job as director and executive producer of *It's Always Sunny in Philadelphia*. Not to let his academic skills lag, he founded the well-reviewed Black Dahlia Theater in Los Angeles, a nonprofit organization that aims to develop and produce new plays by both well-known and up-and-coming writers. Matt has used his talents and abilities to maintain a balanced life in the sometimes cutthroat world of entertainment while helping others along their own theatrical paths.

HEIDI ZEIGLER

(Born March 26, 1979)

Character: Sherry Lubbock

Heidi had a strong career as a child actor but decided to retire after her last role as a lead in the 1991 series *Drexell's Class,* starring Dabney Coleman. She was chosen as Sherry, the youngest daughter in *Just the Ten of Us*, after she had appeared in the series *Rags to Riches* for one season, two episodes of *Growing Pains,* and other acting jobs. Opting for a private and more academic life, Heidi received her BS and then multiple graduate degrees by studying at BYU, USD, and SDSU. Not all ex–child stars have to continue acting. Many have found fulfilling and successful lives in other forms of business than show.

JASON KORSTJENS
JEREMY KORSTJENS

(Twins born in 1988)

Character: Harvey Lubbock

Yes, twins always seemed to get listed together—well, after all, they are playing just one character—unless they are fraternal twins. Toddler Harvey was just in two seasons, and all three of them (the character Harvey, Jason, and Jeremy) called it quits in 1990 after their brief foray in the wonderful world of showbiz. They now can be found on the competitive foosball circuit competing in another form of entertainment.

Roseanne

9 Seasons: 222 episodes

Network: ABC; Color

Debut: October 18, 1988 / Finale: May 20, 1997

Roseanne brought blue-collar comedy back into style when her self-titled sitcom debuted in the fall of 1988. An immediate hit, the show struck a note with viewers because it featured a "normal" family with financial challenges, weight issues, and behavioral problems. Over the course of nine seasons, *Roseanne* explored cultural and social issues in a manner not seen since the Norman Lear years.

SARA GILBERT

(Born January 29, 1975)

Character: Darlene Conner

Sara, younger sister of Melissa from *Little House on the Prairie*, followed in her adopted sister's footsteps when all the hoopla surrounding Melissa getting a star

The cast of *Roseanne*, Season 9. Shown from left: Glenn Quinn, Michael Fishman, Johnny Galecki, Sara Gilbert, Martin Mull, Roseanne Barr, Estelle Parsons, John Goodman, Laurie Metcalf, Sarah Chalke, 1996.
ABC/Photofest

on the Walk of Fame in Hollywood inspired her to join the family acting troupe. She wanted to be an actress, too, and began by doing commercials that segued into appearances on episodic television and TV-movies. While she was on *Roseanne,* she interspersed her acting with studies at Yale University, from which she graduated in 1997 with degrees in art and philosophy. After the show she appeared in the movies *High Fidelity* and *Riding in Cars with Boys*. But boys weren't really her pursuit; she had a ten-year relationship with producer/writer Allison Adler and they had two children together, one by Ali and one by Sara, both via sperm donors. Sara reunited with her good friend and love interest on *Roseanne,* Johnny Galecki, to appear in several episodes of *The Big Bang Theory*. She developed and is executive producer of the TV show *The Talk*, which she continues to cohost. Sara is now married to singer Linda Perry, and they have one son, whom Sara bore at forty. This is an ex–child star with a mind and heart of her own.

MICHAEL FISHMAN

(Born October 22, 1981)

Character: D. J. Conner

Michael is another child star who grew up in front of the camera. At age six he was awarded a regular role in *Roseanne*. He had a good experience, saying, "I was a happy kid living a dream surrounded by great people on *Roseanne*." And in another interview, "As a child actor it's important to follow the examples of people like Ron Howard and Jodie Foster who not only have been successful as adults but as members of society." After the show, Michael continued acting in some TV episodics, started college, but followed his sports leanings and played baseball with Mexican and Japanese teams. He then transitioned to behind-the-scenes writing and producing. Michael married his wife, Jennifer, in 1999, and they have two children. When his good friend Glenn Quinn, an actor from *Roseanne*, died, Michael's spirit moved him to reenter acting; he has since continued to take interesting roles that suit him and give back to his community through his contributions to many charities. He also coaches baseball and softball for underprivileged kids and has shown that stereotypes of muddled ex–child stars can be blatantly false.

LECY GORANSON

(Born June 22, 1974)

Character: Becky Conner I

Lecy stayed with *Roseanne* for six seasons before she, as given name Alicia, went off to Vassar to attend college. Whereas the production company shot scenes with Sara Gilbert on campus when she attended Yale, Alicia opted for the entire university experience and would be seen intermittently on phone conversations. The company under the guidance of Roseanne emphasized education to their young acting charges, and the child stars benefited greatly from this attitude. Alicia did come back for the eighth season to share acting duties with Sarah Chalke, who had taken over as Becky when Alicia left, but she was totally back to her studies for the final year. *Roseanne* was Lecy's first foray into show business. After the series and her graduation from college, she appeared in television shows but claims her real passion is acting in theatre. Explaining why she needed to go off to college, Alicia said, "At that time, I craved normalcy."

SARAH CHALKE

(Born August 27, 1976)

Character: Becky Conner II

Sarah took over the role of Becky when Alicia's studies at Vassar and her involvement in the college rugby team started usurping more of her time. The two Beckys were never explained to the audiences, but sly references were made on occasion, like "Oh, you here this week?" Sarah was eight years old when she stepped onto the boards of a theatrical musical. As a Canadian she starred in *KidZone* as a reporter and then she jumped onto the successful US series bandwagon as the second Becky. Sarah said of her experience on the show: "I think being on *Roseanne* didn't just help my career—it gave me my career." Her success has since included the starring role on TV's *Scrubs* as Dr. Elliot Reed and on three short-lived TV series. In 2015 she was tapped to costar in the comedy *48 Hours 'til Monday* with Rob Riggle. Sarah has appeared on the big screen in *Chaos Theory* and *Mama's Boy*. She has a son by lawyer Jamie Afifi (Sarah's father is also a lawyer). Sarah, like other progeny from *Roseanne,* volunteers much of her time to worthwhile charities; good models are very important to impressionable child actors.

JOHNNY GALECKI

(Born April 30, 1975)
Character: David Healy

Johnny, like Sarah, has enjoyed a successful *Roseanne* afterlife. He started his child acting career at twelve when he appeared with JoBeth Williams and his future *Roseanne* costar John Goodman in the CBS TV-movie *Murder Ordained.* He also tucked the role of Rusty Griswold under his movie belt in the popular movie *National Lampoon's Christmas Vacation.* After he became the love interest of Becky in *Roseanne*, he went on to a film career, starring in such films as *I Know What You Did Last Summer* and *Suicide Kings.* His second break in the series world came when he was cast in *The Big Bang Theory,* in the role of Leonard Hofstadter. He has been paid royally for his excellent skills on this series. Johnny is quite an eligible bachelor but has spent much of his off time developing his 360 acres of land in Santa Margarita, California. Who says being an ex–child star is such a bad deal?

Family Matters

9 Seasons: 215 episodes

Network: ABC (1989–97), CBS (1997–98); Color

Debut: September 22, 1989 / Finale: July 17, 1998

Family Matters was a spin-off of the then-popular sitcom *Perfect Strangers*. The original premise focused on a blended working class African-American family, and the Winslow family might not matter today had it not been for the talented breakout character of next-door neighbor Steve Urkel, delightfully portrayed by Jaleel White. This domestic sitcom had all the standard plot devices viewers were familiar with, except for one major difference—once the clumsy, snorting, nerdishly brilliant Steve Urkel got mixed up in the situation, there was no telling how far and fast things could spiral out of control. Lucille Ball would have been proud.

The cast of *Family Matters*. Shown standing: Darius McCrary, Jaleel White; seated: Kellie Shanygne Williams, Bryton McClure, JoMarie Payton Noble, Reginald VelJohnson, Rosetta LeNoire.

ABC/Photofest

JALEEL WHITE

(Born November 27, 1976)
Character: Steve Urkel

Jaleel made quite an impression on everyone when he appeared in the first season of *Family Mattters* as a guest star and became the most memorable character of this long-running series. He had an early start in showbiz with a commercial for Jell-O Pops with Bill Cosby. Later on he was considered for a role in Bill's show, but the comedian had a change of heart and turned the part into one for a girl. After his long stint on *Family Matters*, Jaleel was of course expected to act like Urkel, so directors were pleasantly surprised to find out that he could easily don another character. Jaleel has acted in many roles on TV and in movies, and he is known for his voice creation of Sonic the Hedgehog in various animated incarnations of this character. A UCLA graduate in film, he wrote, produced, and starred in a web series, hosted the game show *Total Blackout*, and waltzed on *Dancing with the Stars* Season 14. Jaleel continues to find his successful way in the show business realm, and has been quoted as saying that "he looks at his decade-long portrayal of Urkel as training for his career as director, writer, and actor." What an excellent way to look at ex–childhood stardom!

KELLIE SHANYGNE WILLIAMS

(Born March 22, 1976)
Character: Laura Winslow

It's always good to have a strong family behind you in this business. Kellie's dad took a video of her and sent it in as her audition tape for *Family Matters*. From the age of six, she had gained experience acting in theatrical presentations on the East Coast, but she then moved to Los Angeles for her work on the series. After the show Kellie matriculated from UCLA. She continued to act in TV parts and produced a movie called *Blessed and Cursed*. About her roles after *Family Matters,* she has stated, "You get lazy being on a sitcom for so long." I agree that some of the incentive and energy is drained from child star graduates of TV. Kellie married Hannibal Jackson in 2009, and they have two children. Today Kellie's biggest roles, besides speaker and contributor to many charities, are those of devoted wife and mother. She always was a family-oriented person.

DARIUS McCRARY

(Born May 1, 1976)

Character: Eddie Winslow

Darius has continued his child-acting stardom and expanded it to include music production and songwriting. His father was a gospel jazz musician and an early influence on his child's career. Darius made his film debut in *Big Shots* followed by an excellent performance in *Mississippi Burning*. After the series, he costarred with Whoopi Goldberg in the film *Kingdom Come*, captured a three-season run on *The Young and the Restless* and then a recurring part on the TV series *Anger Management*. He has released a CD and continues to write music. The music business may not be as substantial as TV stardom, because Darius was arrested in 2015 for nonpayment of child support for his only daughter. Family does matter, Darius.

BRYTON JAMES

(Born August 17, 1986)
Character: Richie Crawford

Bryton made his show business debut on *Family Matters* in the second season at the age of three. He was billed as Bryton McClure, his name at birth. Growing up on the show, he gained much valuable experience to help him garner new roles after the show's run ended in 1998. In 2001 he took a short hiatus and signed on as a singer with Polydor/Universal. But he returned to acting, grabbing the role of Corey in *The Intruders* and securing parts in *The Vampire Diaries* and *Heroes* before finding longevity in the soap opera *The Young and the Restless*, where he met up with former costar Darius McCrary. He was married for three years to Ashley Leisinger before they divorced. Bryton continues in the acting world, looking for his next big part.

JAIMEE FOXWORTH

(Born December 17, 1979)
Character: Judy Winslow

Jaimee was unceremoniously dropped from *Family Matters* in the fourth season. Various reasons have been given, such as Steve Urkel's rise, lack of production money, and the like, but it had a devastating effect on young Jaimee both financially and psychologically. Without funds and depressed, she began a downward spiral into drugs and alcohol abuse. She tried to form a music group with her sisters, but failing at that she entered the pornographic world and made a number of films under the pseudonym of Crave. When she became pregnant by her boyfriend, she had an awakening and vowed to stop smoking marijuana and drink less. When a healthy baby boy was born to her, she began to get her life together, appearing on reality shows like *Celebrity Rehab with Dr. Drew* and *Life After*. She has started to rise above her former tumultuous circumstances.

Summation

Having done research for this book, having worked with many of the ex–child stars mentioned, and being an ex–child actor myself, I gathered insight as to how some were able to escape typecasting and stigma and become successful adults and how others encountered seemingly insurmountable roadblocks, which added to the unflattering stereotype.

There are elements shared by many of the successful ex–child actors, the ones who were able to make the transition to either acting in adulthood or walking some other satisfying life path.

For one, the parents of the successful ex–child actors did not use their minor children's income to pay parental bills or support other members of the family. Many times, the parents of child actors used their progeny's earnings to overpay for business expenses or they installed themselves as managers so they could collect a salary. When this happened, all the money that the children earned could easily disappear. Child actors in these circumstances entered adulthood not only penniless but also bitter, which often led to substance abuse, broken hearts, broken homes, and worse.

SUMMATION

One element shared by successful teenage and young adult actors is that they did not get hooked on drugs and alcohol. Or when they did, they managed to find the right support to overcome their bad habits before their habits overcame them.

Education played a large part in the confidence, success, and happiness of those ex–child actors who cherished their past experiences and went on to find new ones. Formal education allowed young people to proceed with a foundation for further understanding of the life process, whether or not they go into new fields of study.

Advice in making meaningful choices given by strong family members, mentors, or other reliable guides helped many of the ex–child stars. Professional financial advice, when followed, gave the young adults a firm monetary foundation, so when times got rough and they were not securing parts, there was something else of substance to support them.

Good self-esteem ranked high among the ex–child stars who flourished and very low among those who didn't. A sudden downward spiral from the pinnacle of success is difficult for a youngster to accept. Was it his fault? Did she not do a good enough job? These questions can haunt children. Without psychological help or family support, an abrupt change in lifestyle can lead to emotional and financial disabilities that can last a lifetime.

I also believe there is a consciousness in many of the ex–child stars that can be expressed as, "I was successful once. Isn't that good enough? Do I really have to put myself out there again to be judged, to be criticized, even if it is what I enjoy doing?" There seems to be a lack of incentive, drive, or desire to find their dream. They already experienced the dream when they were children. They feel entitled to the same treatment they received as children, and some can't get past those childish expectations that they should be waited on, catered to, and believed in all they say or demand. The feeling also persists that since they were stars as children, they should only take on starring parts. They do not consider that many of them were hired because they were cute, not because of their innate acting ability. They certainly learn from their experiences on camera, but still, those experiences do not amount to formal acting training.

So when a series ends, teenagers who hold out for starring jobs—especially before they reach the age of eighteen and can work longer hours—are really narrowing their professional work and choices. Then, not finding any starring jobs and unwilling to take supporting roles, they feel depressed; I think that is why so many give up and leave the business.

Many of them also believe they were victims who find themselves in their current situation because of what someone did to them when they were young and defenseless. That may be true, but difficult things happen to children in many walks of life. And that type of victimization rhetoric hurts more than helps the child actor to get over the past and move on. The understanding that they are now adults and can make life what they choose it to be must be emphasized to them.

There are many interesting paths to follow, trials to be forgotten, and moments to be embraced as they live their ex-child-star lives today. There are many rewards in being a young celebrity and yet many risks as well. Disney instituted a policy that children/'tweens who are contracted to work or star in a series for the company must go to the Disney psychologist once a week to discuss feelings, problems, and concerns. They are given advice on how to handle fame and the myriad demands on their time and psyche. Especially now with social media blasting someone's clothing choice or any errant blemish that might appear on an otherwise flawless complexion, young stars need to beware of the scope of the criticism and how to handle it.

If difficulties are not properly confronted, the chance of using numbing medications, legal or illegal, developing a hard cynical edge, or developing into a depressive personality is heightened. There should be prehab so there won't be rehab. There should be help available for all these talented children.

SUMMATION

Paul Petersen, with his A Minor Consideration organization, has gone far in helping with the financial aspects of child labor. His efforts have led some states to require the establishment of "Coogan accounts" so that a percentage of a child's earnings can only be redeemed by the child when he or she turns eighteen. But when the teenager gets the money, he or she still needs guidance; too many have received their money and blown it all in two weeks. Perhaps there could be a financial advisory attached to the redemption of the money, to provide guidance to newly minted young adults on how best to save, invest, and spend some of their hard-earned gains.

A Minor Consideration also operates as a support group, does outreach, and is available to those who are blasted in the media for their behavior or have become entangled in legal webs or are suffering from drug abuse. There are also transitional workshops where actors can go to find out about other aspects of the business to tide them over to their next acting job; they can even find out about jobs to embrace an entirely new outlet for their talents. Workshops on how to direct, produce, be a grip, do public relations, or function as a casting director—all aspects of the business they worked so long in—are offered. Attending college is also emphasized, whether it be a community college, online institution, or other academic outlet, to help the ex–child star experience other aspects of life.

Yes, sometimes it is great to be a child star. This book has shown where some of them have gone wrong and where some of them have achieved unmitigated success. A new batch of young, talented actors can shine with the right training, care, and attention. It is important and necessary to help these talented fledglings stay on a supported path to avoid the potentially debilitating Hollywood quagmire. Our national treasures deserve nurturing, and those of us who know the ropes are here for them!

Acknowledgments

So many people to thank, so little time. The first accolade goes to Manny Cabacungan Jr., the wind beneath Kathy's and Fred's wings in the preparation of this book. He must have been lonely in our shadows, but he never let on. He was instrumental in gathering the first round of photos that grace this book and helped make it so outstanding.

Kudos to our literary agent par excellence Melissa McComas and her team at Tsunami Productions for going beyond the usual expectations and using her time to get *X Child Stars* off and running the perfect literary marathon.

A great big thank you to the Rowman & Littlefield squad for help in energetically passing the finished book to the goal line: Rick Rinehart for making sure all was done according to his high bar, always proficient editor Evan Helmlinger for keeping his eye and hands on the ball and in directing the right permissions and photos to the place where they should be, Meredith Dias for overseeing the project, and Helen Subbio for her excellent copyediting.

ACKNOWLEDGMENTS

The X Child Stars—the national treasures who are never forgotten and remain forever in the hearts and memories of untold millions of fans and TV viewers around the world.

Kathy's family—David, Reid, and Megan—the support team who understood, loved, and held down the fort in the torrential whirlwind of a busy schedule in getting this book written and to press while Kathy was performing on TV and films and promoting her autobiography, *Surviving Cissy: My Family Affair of Life in Hollywood*, at the same time!

Fred's sister, Valerie, is much appreciated for keeping the light and spirit of her and Fred's mother glowing and for reminding him he can accomplish anything he puts his mind to.

Index

INDEX

INDEX

INDEX

INDEX

INDEX

INDEX

INDEX

INDEX

DATE DUE

JUL 1 0 2017		
JUL 2 4 2017		
JUL 2 6 2017		
		PRINTED IN U.S.A.